# God's Way

# God's Way.

## Paul Bassett

EVANGELICAL PRESS

EVANGELICAL PRESS
16/18 High Street, Welwyn, Hertfordshire, AL6 9EQ,
England

© Evangelical Press 1981
*First published 1981*

ISBN 0 85234 147 4

Typeset by Solo Typesetting, Maidstone, Kent.
Printed in the U.S.A.

# Contents

|                          | Page |
|--------------------------|------|
| Preface                  | 7    |
| 1. God-given gospel      | 9    |
| 2. God-given agency      | 33   |
| 3. God-given pattern     | 62   |
| 4. God-given proclamation| 78   |
| 5. God-given direction   | 94   |
| 6. God-given vision      | 112  |
| 7. God-given compassion  | 123  |
| 8. God-given prayer      | 133  |

# Preface

My sole purpose in writing the book is to record an impassioned and, I pray, biblically reasoned plea to return to New Testament methods of evangelism, especially focusing on the local church as God's chosen agency. It is my very definite conviction that individual Christians are not witnessing for God as fearlessly and as faithfully as did their predecessors in past ages, and that ministers need more and more to do 'the work of an evangelist'. But, perhaps most of all, this book encourages us to pray for the forgotten gift of an evangelist working from the basis of our local churches. I believe many of us have sat too long in the seat of the critic and have been rebuked by Moody's supposed retort: 'My something is better than your nothing.' May this book stir us to identify ourselves with the Master Evangelist and determine with Him that 'I must work the works of him that sent me, while it is day: the night cometh, when no man can work. As long as I am in the world, I am the light of the world' (John 9:4,5).

PAUL BASSETT

## Acknowledgement

I wish to record my thanks to Gordon Sayer, the Librarian of the Evangelical Library, and his staff for their assistance, to David Ide for the help received from his own private library, and also to Miss Margery Ellson who has typed and retyped this manuscript. Their help has been greatly appreciated.

# 1
# God-given gospel

Have you ever paused in the midst of the rush of life to ask
God a question: 'What is the most beautiful thing in the
world?' He answers, it is the beautiful proclamation of salvation. It is a man sent from God, preaching peace to a
world without peace, announcing salvation to a sinful
world. It is a man saved by God's grace, preaching that
grace to lost mankind. Whether that message fell in ancient
times from the lips of prophet or apostle, or whether it
falls today from my lips or yours, I believe God still says,
'How beautiful!' I wonder how many times a day God has
reason to utter those two words: 'How beautiful!' I know
the answer to that question. Whenever and wherever in the
world a man declares to his fellow man the gospel of God's
salvation, God still says, 'How beautiful!' God does not
utter these words about some impassioned plea by a lawyer
or an impressive oration by a statesman; no, only about a
man preaching God. For ultimately this is the only message
that matters to God, since it is the restoration of God's
beauty to the ugliness of man's world. It is the restoration
of the image of God in man, which was ruined by the Fall.

## Restored masterpiece

It must be a wonderful sight to see an artist restoring an
apparently ruined and marred masterpiece to its original
glory. How much time and patience he spends on it, until
finally the original magnificent image is restored! Yet as I
observe God working in the life of a man I see in an even
greater sense the restoration of a ruin to an original master-

piece. The purpose of evangelism is nothing less than the
restoration of the ruined image of God in man.

You see, man has lived so long with the ruin of his life
that he has forgotten his original glory and sinlessness. His
ears have been deaf too long to those wondrous words of
the three glorious Artists of the Godhead: 'Let *us* make
man in *our* image, after *our* likeness' (Gen. 1:26). Here was
the very climax of God's creative work — a man created in
the image and likeness of God! In the decision to create
man and in the creative act itself the Father, the Son and
the Holy Spirit were all equally at work to produce God's
masterpiece. At that moment, if we had been permitted to
enter God's gallery to view His masterpiece, we should
have said of Adam, God's first man, 'Isn't he like God? Isn't
he like his Father? Isn't he like God's Son? Isn't he like
God's Spirit? Indeed, he is the very image of God!'

But if we then let our eyes move downwards and look at
modern man and, indeed, at ourselves, we have to ask,
'What has happened to man? What has happened to me?
Where is that glorious image and likeness of the original
Creator, God? 'Why,' we may well ask, 'are we confronted
on every side with this marred and ruined image of God in
man?' In a word, God's answer is that man has sinned. Man
has ruined his righteousness by rebelling against his Maker.
He is now only a marred and fallen image of God. God's
own history book of man relates how, sadly, His glorious
image and likeness in man crashed in one fatal moment:
'As by one man sin entered into the world . . .' (Rom. 5:12).

Yet how comforting and encouraging it is to look away
from what man has ruined to what God can restore! The
restorer is no less a person than God's only Son. One writer
in the Bible describes Him as 'the brightness of his glory'
(Heb. 1:3). The word 'brightness' conveys the idea of daybreak. Indeed, the coming of Christ from heaven to earth
was God's daybreak, the dawning of a new day of hope for
man. In Christ, God's sun shines in a world darkened by
sin. He is most perfectly described as 'the Sun of righteousness [risen] with healing in his wings' (Mal. 4:2). But Christ
is above all else 'the express image' of God's person, and it

is only when ruined man looks at Christ with the eye of faith that he can begin to realize what he has lost through sin. By faith he sees for the first time 'the image of God'. He begins to see what man was once like and what he can become again. But he also sees God, for he sees Christ 'who is the image of the invisible God' (Col. 1:15). How wonderful it is that Christ can make visible the invisible God!

It is only when man looks back to his beginning that he realizes that even his personality is part of that image and likeness of God. Those three glorious Persons of the Godhead who declared, 'Let *us* make man in *our* image and after *our* likeness', permitted something of Their personality to be created in man. For man is a person as God is three Persons. Sadly, sin has blinded him to this glorious gift of personality that distinguishes him from everything else in God's creation. In a day when man considers the individual unimportant, we need to realize that every person whom God created matters to God. Secondly, man, by his sin, has marred that original goodness which was once part of the image of God in man, for once God looked upon man 'and, behold, God saw everything that he made, and it was *very* good'! How very far we have all fallen from that image!

Finally, there is only one hope for man, and that is to come back to the God who originally made him in His image. We have too long been blinded to our true state. It is a great day for the sinner, in his ruined and hopeless condition, when he stumbles upon these words: 'But if our gospel be hid, it is hid to them that are lost: in whom the god of this world hath blinded the minds of them which believe not, lest the light of the glorious gospel of Christ, who is the image of God, should shine unto them.' The restoring spiritual light of God is just as wonderful as the light that dawned at creation. Paul's words to the Corinthians apply just as much to us today: 'God, who commanded the light to shine out of darkness, hath shined in our hearts, to give *the light of the knowledge of the glory of God* in the face of Jesus Christ' (2 Cor. 4:3,4,6).

The man Isaiah is describing when he uses the words:

'How beautiful!' (Isa. 52:7; Rom. 10:15) is someone who brings good news, who has evidently carried his message over a great distance and at a great personal cost to himself, perhaps scaling mountain peaks and traversing deserts on his way. At last he reaches his destination. No doubt to the messenger himself at that moment his feet appear black and bleeding, even ugly, but to the recipient of the message they are the most beautiful feet in the world, because they have brought God Himself and His message of peace with God and salvation from sin. Unless our feet become feet like that God will never say of us, our places of worship or the way we spend our time, 'How beautiful!' God uses 'beauty' as another word for evangelism. True evangelism in God's estimation is a thing of great beauty and we, the people of God, the church of God in our generation, must arrive at the same conclusion.

## Manual of evangelism

Before even the need for a consideration of fresh opportunities for evangelism, there must first come a new awareness of God. We must turn again to His manual of evangelism, the Bible, and His provision for the work of evangelism. We will then immediately discover that God, with His own perfect economy of language, has reduced His message to mankind to one human yet divinely inspired Word. This Word is expressed in the language of the world in which it was given, but it is a world Word because it is a world-wide message. It is an international Word because it is a message to people of every language, tribe and nation. It is a good Word to a bad world. It is gospel, good news, *(evangelion)*. It is a Word into which God Himself has entered and through which He has travelled to His lost world. It is therefore a person-to-person Word. It is a living Word. It is a Word pregnant with God and His saving goodness towards evil and godless men. Evangelism is not therefore man's message about God, but God's message about Himself. Again, it is not a message conveying the possibility of good news, but the certainty of it. It is intrinsically, dynamically and powerfully good, God's instrument of goodness to a perishing world. Evangelism is the good news (the evangel) in action: a man caught in the act of proclaiming that message to mankind.

To understand the origin of true evangelism, therefore, we must begin with God and not with man; with the sinless and not with the sinful. The movement of evangelism is from eternity into time, from heaven to earth, from God to man, and then through man to mankind. Before God had ordained or appointed a messenger or preacher, He 'appointed' Himself. Before He sent a prophet or apostle, He 'sent' Himself. As the gospel is God Himself, so the first preacher was God Himself. In the glorious open-air pulpit of 'paradise lost' we hear the first Preacher preaching the first sermon in this world, calling lost man and woman back to Himself: 'The seed of the woman shall bruise the serpent's heel' (Gen. 3:15). As God directly preached the first gospel sermon to Adam and Eve, so He did to Abraham, the future father of all faithful believers. As the theme of God's first sermon was the message of the cross, Christ's victory over Satan, so His theme to Abraham was justification by faith alone. Yes, God Himself preached the doctrine of justification, before Habakkuk, Paul or Luther. The brief New Testament record of it declares, 'And the scripture, foreseeing that God would justify the heathen through faith, preached before the gospel unto Abraham, saying, In thee shall all nations be blessed' (Gal. 3:8). Though these two sermons were initially addressed to individuals, they convey a message to all mankind throughout time. They were international in their scope, declaring that the reality of man's future happiness or blessedness was dependent on his personal saving faith in God's gospel of salvation. Here we find the very basis and heart of evangelism. The gospel derives its authority from the Scriptures alone and it is to be received through faith alone. It is also God's *only* message to be preached to a heathen world.

## Unchanging message

As we open our New Testament, we hear the door of John

the Baptist's prison closing and at the same moment the
voice of Christ speaking. God is using a different messenger
but the same message: 'From that time Jesus began to
preach, and to say, Repent: for the kingdom of heaven is at
hand' (Matt. 4:17; 3:1,2). Man must repent because the
King Himself is standing at the door of the world. Man's
mind must be changed in relation to God. Repentance
requires knowledge of sin as well as of salvation. It calls for
both conviction of sin and confession to God. The reign of
the King of kings must replace that of Satan and sin.
Repentance for our sin leads to receiving the King into our
lives. But if we would come to the heart of the gospel, we
must consider the unique day in the history of the world,
when God's own Son rose triumphant over sin, death and
hell. It was the day of God's triumph over the terrible
triumvirate of man's tormentors. Yet man himself remained
for a time ignorant of God's glorious victory on his behalf.
He remained a fool and an unbeliever. For the disciples
considered the early morning 'news headlines' of the resurrection of Christ 'idle tales, and they believed them not'
(Luke 24:11). If that fact fills our modern minds with
incredulity, can you imagine walking seven or eight miles
in deep conversation with God and yet remaining totally
ignorant of the identity of the risen Lord? Yet these are
the facts of history.

The evangelism of that resurrection evening took place
along a road somewhere between the city of Jerusalem and
the village of Emmaus. Suddenly even God can stand it no
longer. The voice of Christ fills the evening air with justifi-
able indignation and righteous rebuke: 'O fools, and slow
of heart to believe all that the prophets have spoken: ought
not Christ to have suffered these things, and to enter into
his glory?' (Luke 24: 25,26). He preached to those who
still believed Christ to be dead and not alive, absent and
not present. His rebuke, therefore, is addressed to our ears
as much as to theirs, and to our day as well as theirs. No
doubt the smell of the grave was still upon Christ, no doubt
He could have pointed to His nail-pierced hands and feet as
undeniable and irrefutable proofs of His sacrifice and His

passion. But the finger of God that day pointed, not downwards to the imprint of the nails, but backwards to the pages of the Psalms and Prophets. The beginning is sin and the ending is salvation from sin. Evangelism must begin where Christ begins. For Christ preached that resurrection evening, 'beginning at Moses and all the prophets, he expounded unto them in all the scriptures the things concerning himself' (Luke 24:27). How quickly men had forgotten the dying words of Christ, uttered merely three days before! Modern man, too, has forgotten that at the heart of history there is a cross, and that the crucifixion is the fulfilment of four thousand years of prophetic history. Mankind has forgotten the dying word of Christ: 'Finished!' (John 19:30.)

## Dying in triumph

The dying words of any man are always listened to and heeded. They are stored away in the archives of memory, sometimes never to be forgotten. If this is true of mere man, how much more should this be true of the dying words of the Son of God! This dying word of Christ was not whispered from a deathbed, but cried out on a cross of agony. In the original it stands as a single word of triumph. 'Finished!' was the message which echoed from Calvary. The word in the Greek is in the perfect tense which describes an action brought to its appropriate conclusion, yet in such a way that its results still remain in action. The cross of Christ is a past fact of history, yet it is also a present power in this world. We may well ask what we know of that power in our lives. Do we really believe that Christ has finished, for time and eternity, all that is necessary for the salvation of our souls?

Firstly, He has finished *His Father's work*. When Christ died at Calvary nearly two thousand years ago, He was, above all else, finishing His Father's work — one which His Father had planned in eternity. God knew that the man whom He was going to create would sin against Him and would require a Saviour to die for him. Christ was delivered

up to die, not by man, but by His loving Father. For our
Bible tells us, 'Him, being delivered by the determinate
counsel and foreknowledge of God, ye have taken, and by
wicked hands have crucified and slain' (Acts 2:23). Christ
was always conscious of performing His Father's will.
Early in His ministry He revealed this fact when He said,
'My meat is to do the will of him that sent me, and to finish
his work' (John 4:34). Men did not realize this, but Satan
did, and tried to make Christ do anything rather than die
on the cross. Once, he tempted Him to turn stones into
bread. Another time, he attempted to make Him leap off
the temple. Finally, he offered Him the world instead of
the cross. Satan knew that, once Christ was on the cross,
his own power was gone and he would be conquered by
Christ. So great was the love of Christ for us sinners, and
so set was He on finishing His Father's work, that He 'stead-
fastly set His face toward Jerusalem', the place for His
finished work. Shortly before going to the cross we hear
Him pray to His Father, 'I have glorified thee on the earth:
I have finished the work which thou gavest me to do' (John
17:4). The death of Christ upon the cross, far from being
the frustration of His Father's work, was in fact the finishing of it! It was not simply a life taken by man, but rather
a life given by God for man.

Secondly, He finished and fulfilled *the sacrifices of the
Old Testament* which pointed forwards to, and typified
Him. So the apostle Paul sees in the sacrifice of Christ at
Calvary the final Passover Lamb. He remembers how the
children of Israel killed the lamb, as God had commanded,
and as a result of sprinkling the blood on their houses they
saw the judgement of God 'pass over' them. Paul, therefore,
describes the sacrifice of the Lord Jesus, saying, 'Christ
our passover is sacrificed for us' (1 Cor. 5:7). He sees that
the last Lamb of God has been slain. John, in his Gospel,
goes on to reveal that the purpose of the finished work is
that we 'behold the Lamb of God, which taketh away the
sin of the world' (John 1:29). Christ was finishing the way
of salvation for sinners, which the sacrifices of the Old
Testament never could accomplish. The writer to the

Hebrews reminds us, 'For it is not possible that the blood of bulls and of goats should take away sins' (Heb. 10:4).

Thirdly, Christ finished and fulfilled *the prophecies of the Old Testament* with regard to salvation. The first book of the Bible informs us that, in the very place where man sinned against God, God gave a prophecy of a Saviour from sin. He spoke of the cross and the finished work of salvation when he said that the seed of the woman would bruise the serpent's head (Gen. 3:15). The words echo down through the centuries and, a few hundred years before Christ's death, we read, 'Thou shalt make his soul an offering for sin' (Isa. 53:10). As we open the Bible at Psalm 22 we find there foretold the cry of anguish uttered by our Saviour on the cross: 'My God, My God, why hast thou forsaken me?' (Matt. 27:46.)

Finally, and above all, we must realize personally that Christ finished *the work of man's salvation*. If there is one word which we need to hear today it is this triumphant cry: 'Finished!' The majority of people in Britain are living as if Christ had never died. They imply that the work of salvation was not finished by Christ. What is Christianity for the majority? It is trying to make ourselves good enough for God, trying to live a good life. That is as good as saying that Christ's sacrifice was not sufficient to save us from sin, to make us fit for heaven and acceptable with God. It is essential that we pay heed to these words: 'By one offering He hath perfected for ever them that are sanctified' (Heb. 10:14), and, again, 'Now once in the end of the world hath he appeared to put away sin by the sacrifice of himself' (Heb. 9:26). His work was to die for our sins, and that work is finished for ever. Ours is to repent of our sins and to believe that He died for us.

Returning to the resurrection day, we see Christ made it the 'link-day' between ancient and modern times. It was intended to be a day not only of new life for His church, but also one of new understanding. Indeed, we see that Christ enlightened His apostles as to the history of the gospel before commissioning them to introduce a new era of gospel history. On that resurrection day Christ also made Himself the 'link-Man' between prophet and apostle. In Himself He introduced the apostles to the prophets, and in a unique moment of history handed over to the apostles the gospel which they were to preach. Only then did they become His 'sent ones', rooted in Christ, in Scripture and in history, with Christ's immortal commission ringing in their ears: 'Thus it is *written,* and thus it behoved Christ to suffer, and to rise from the dead the third day: and that repentance and remission of sins should be preached in his name among all nations, beginning at Jerusalem. And ye are witnesses of these things' (Luke 24:46-48). We see here in Christ's words the centrality of preaching, as the method of evangelism to all nations, and the centrality of the death and resurrection of Christ, as the message of the gospel.

## Which side of the cross?

The New Testament church knew nothing of this twentieth-century 'Christianity' which has a cross in the church but no cross in the sermon. The early church knew of no salvation apart from the crucifixion. How far the church today, generally speaking, has strayed from Calvary!

The apostle Paul declared, 'For the preaching of the cross is to them that perish foolishness; but unto us which are saved it is the power of God' (1 Cor. 1:18). Do we not need to seek the answer to the hymn which asks, 'Oh teach *me* what it meaneth, that cross uplifted high'? The cross is God's sword which divides all men into two groups: those who think the cross is foolishness and those who think it is the power of God. There is no neutrality concerning the cross of Christ. Our attitude to the cross determines our attitude to Christ. It tells us whether we are Christians or not. Our reaction towards Christ dying on the cross nearly two thousand years ago is a description of our present spiritual condition today. Anyone who thinks that the cross is a foolish thing is not only passing a judgement about Christ, but at the same time about himself or herself. 'For', we read, 'the preaching of the cross is to them that perish foolishness.' It is only a perishing soul that considers

the dying sacrifice of Christ to be folly. To understand
what we mean by 'perishing', we do not need to reach for
the Oxford Dictionary, but for the Word of God. It tells us
that 'God so loved the world, that he gave his only begotten
Son, that whosoever believeth in him should not perish,
but have everlasting life'. So the word 'perishing' describes
the state of a man's soul who has not believed in Christ; it
is the opposite to everlasting life. To perish is to live and
die without Christ and without everlasting life. It is the
saddest sight, surely, in the world to see a man perishing in
his sin, yet blind to the Saviour who came to save him
from that state. He sees the cross as a foolish thing, because
his sin has blinded him to the fact that the cross is God's
wisdom. Man may in some degree see the wisdom of God
demonstrated in the creation of the world, but yet remain
totally blind to God's supreme display of wisdom in the
dying sacrifice of His Son.

We may well ask what was God's purpose in revealing
His wisdom to the world in such a way. He tells us, 'For it
is written, I will destroy the wisdom of the wise.' It was to
destroy the proud natural wisdom of man. The Greeks were
the wisest people of their day, yet the collective wisdom of
Plato, Socrates and Aristotle never led them to a knowledge
of God. God's purpose was to make the wisest men humble
themselves before the cross. God purposely therefore chose
a thing which was foolish and absurd to the wise of this
world: 'For after that in the wisdom of God the world by
wisdom knew not God, it pleased God by the foolishness
of preaching to save them that believe.' A better translation
would be 'It pleased God by the foolishness of the thing
preached [that is, the cross] to save them that believe.'

This leads us naturally to consider the second category
of men found in relation to the cross: 'But unto us which
are saved it is the power of God.' It is interesting to note
at this point that the cross is the greatest demonstration,
not only of the wisdom of God, but also of the power of
God. The power of God used to create the world was not
greater than that which God used to re-create man by
saving him through the cross. It is therefore only 'the saved'

who know the power of God in their lives. The saved man
is the man who has been humbled to see that the cross can
never be understood by natural speculation. It must rather
be accepted by faith as the divine revelation of God's wisdom, love and power to lost man, without Christ, perishing
in his sin. The basic failure of man is that he does not
realize that in God's sight he is perishing in sin and in need
of a Saviour. The cross is there to tell us that we are sinners.
If man had not sinned, there would never have been a cross.
The cross is, therefore, meaningless to me until I recognize
that I am a sinner in God's sight and need a Saviour. It is
only then that I learn that I do not have the power to over-
come sin in my own life, but by faith must appropriate
and lay hold of the power of God revealed in the cross.
The Greek word used for 'power' is the word from which
we arrive at our word 'dynamite'. The precious blood of
Christ poured forth on the cross is still dynamic over the
power and the pollution of sin in our lives. It will not only
cleanse us from past, present and future sin, but it will lead
us on to say with the apostle of old, 'God forbid that I
should glory, save in the cross of our Lord Jesus Christ, by
whom the world is crucified unto me, and I unto the world'
(Gal. 6:14).

### Fact or fiction?

Paul further revealed in his preaching both the historicity
and reliability of Christ's death: 'This is a faithful saying,
and worthy of all acceptation, that Christ Jesus came into
the world to save sinners; of whom I am chief' (1 Tim.
1:15). Paul had proved it to be so experimentally in his
own life. Indeed, a Christian is someone who has proved
God's saying to be *faithful*. The words, 'It is a faithful
saying', can equally well be rendered: 'It is a trustworthy
statement', or 'It is a saying to be trusted', or 'True is the
saying', or 'Reliable is the message'. It is a true statement
about a unique and powerful historical event which took
place in this world. For Paul is describing the death of the
Lord Jesus Christ for sinners, some thirty or more years

after it had taken place. In other words, the passing of the years, rather than having made the apostle doubt the faithfulness of the event, has on the contrary driven him daily for all these years to preach its authenticity. The living, preaching and writing of the apostle may be summarized in his own words: 'For I determined not to know anything among you, save Jesus Christ and him crucified.' Above all else, the apostle knew this to be a faithful saying because it was the saying of a faithful God. The sayings of God are always consistent with the being of God. Time and again Paul writes in his letters, 'God is faithful', or 'God is true.' And even when these words are not explicitly found they are always there by implication. So here we have Paul, inspired by the faithful God, writing down one of God's faithful sayings which has been the subject of his preaching for years.

It is especially important in our day and age to understand why Paul wrote down this faithful saying. It is plainly intended not only for young Timothy and the church of his day, but for the church and the world in every generation as long as time exists, for truth is unchanging and timeless in its relevance and appeal. And the purpose of the saying is revealed in the words: 'Christ Jesus came into the world to save sinners.' The more we study this statement, the more we are forced to believe that God is concerned for the whole of His world. Christianity is not therefore merely a Western faith, but rather God's only message for this world. We are brought to see that there was only one Son of God, and there needed to be only one Saviour, in this whole vast universe, to die for sinners such as us.

Paul went on to declare the implications for man of God's faithful saying. He added, 'And *worthy of all accep-tation.*' This may equally well be translated: 'entitled to the fullest acceptance' or 'deserving of whole-hearted acceptance'. It may truly be said there is no saying in this whole world more worthy of acceptance than this one. It is the faithful saying of the faithful God. It is a trustworthy saying upon which a person's whole life may be cast with confidence. It deserves to be received by all because it is

God's Word. As Paul stresses in his second letter to Timothy,
'All Scripture is given by inspiration of God.' It is not
merely a faithful saying of man about God we are considering, but God speaking faithfully to man and through man.
Yet, in a day when God is said to be dead and His Word is
considered a myth, how blind man is to history! This saying is worthy of our acceptance because it is historically
reliable, which myth never is. There is ample historical
evidence about a certain 'Christ' who lived in Judaea during
the reign of Tiberius, the Roman Emperor (14-37 A.D.).
The historian Tacitus in his *Annals* tells us how Christ
suffered capital punishment by the Roman Procurator,
Pontius Pilate.[1] Suetonius speaks of one who is plainly
Christ[2], and Pliny writes to the Roman Emperor Trajan
that 'Christ' was worshipped by 'the Christians' of Pontus
and Bithynia as their God.[3] All this extra-biblical informa-
tion only goes to confirm the utter faithfulness of the
whole Word of God. Yet, the world today is still largely
blind to this most reliable saying: 'That Christ Jesus came
into the world to save sinners.' Until we consider that
faithful saying worthy of *our* acceptance we will live on in
our sins as if Christ had never come and died for us.

Thirdly, we need to see that this is also a *saving* saying:
'That Christ Jesus came into the world to save sinners.'
What a truly amazing statement this is! By implication it
speaks of the pre-existence of Christ Jesus before He
entered this world, that is, before His wondrous incarnation
and glorious life. But above all it speaks of the sole purpose why the eternal Son of God ever came into such a
world as ours. It describes His descent from heaven to
earth, from God to man, from eternity into time, from
being God to becoming the God-Man. Yet when we look
deeper into the original words we see that the very nature
and condition of all the inhabitants of the world are
described in emphatic terms. For in the original the word
'sinners' is placed side by side with the word 'world'. It
actually reads, 'Christ Jesus came into the world, sinners to
save.' He moved from the realm of holiness into the realm
of sin. God chose to come into a world of sin! For as John

correctly says, 'The whole world lieth in wickedness.' No wonder he describes the response Christ received in such a world in these tragic words: 'And this is the condemnation that light is come into the world but men loved darkness rather than light because their deeds were evil'! If only we could see ourselves as God sees us, then we would realize for the first time in our lives that 'all have sinned and come short of the glory of God,' and that in God's estimation, 'there is none righteous, no not one'.

Now, we may well ask, what made a holy God come into such a world, a world lying in wickedness? Would you have chosen a realm of evil instead of a realm of good? Have you ever heard of a king or a queen choosing to leave their palace for a vile and filthy slum? Such a thing is unheard of. If you say that there must have been a great reason, you are right. It was indeed a great reason by any standards, for it was 'to save sinners'. Did not Paul say of the death of Christ, 'Who gave himself for our sins, that he might deliver us from this present evil world, according to the will of the Father'? If a man looked out of place moving upon the moon's surface, how much more was it out of place for the holy Son of God to sit down with 'publicans and sinners', He who previously had sat down only with holy angels! How out of place it was that He, who eternally had looked upon the face of His Father, should look into the face of sinful men! How out of place it was that God the Son, who once sat upon a throne of glory in heaven, should be nailed to a cross!

He came into this present evil world to deliver us from it by dying for our sins. Behind Paul's words here we hear those of Christ Himself: 'I am not come to call the righteous but sinners to repentance.'

A man will never repent of his sins until he is brought to see that he is not righteous in God's sight and until he sees himself as the sinner Christ came into this world to save. For God says, 'The Son of man came to seek and to save that which was lost.' A man is lost in God's sight until he is found by the Saviour of sinners.

Finally, this faithful saying is a *personal* saying, for Paul

added, 'Of whom I am chief.' If Paul had not believed it to
be a faithful saying, he would not have considered it worthy
to be accepted by him, but he knew that Christ had come
to seek him. And when he looked upon Christ, at that
moment he saw himself as the 'chief of sinners'. Unless this
saying becomes a personal one to us, it will be worthless to
us. At the time of the Reformation in the sixteenth century,
when the Bible was a very rare book in England, a man
called Thomas Bilney bought a Bible and, hiding it under
his coat for fear, he took it to his home. Later, he put into
words how much that Book of books meant to him that
day: 'At the first reading, as I well remember, I chanced
upon this sentence of St Paul (O most sweet and comfortable to my soul!): "It is a true saying and worthy of all
men to be embraced that Jesus Christ came into this world
to save sinners of whom I am chief and principal." This
one sentence through God's instruction and inward working which I did not perceive, did so exhilarate my heart,
being before wounded by the guilt of my sins and being
almost in despair, that immediately I felt a marvellous
comfort and quietness in as much that my bruised bones
leaped for joy.' May each of my readers have a similar
experience to that of Bilney, who was never again the same
man after making this verse his own!

### Everlasting gospel

For many, however, evangelism is still merely a message of
yesterday. By 'yesterday' they mean a few thousand years
ago at the most. No doubt, this is why modern man has
placed the gospel on a par with the so-called gospels of
other religions. It is time that both the professing church
and the disinterested world were made to understand that
when we hear the gospel preached we hear eternity speaking, and when we handle the gospel we handle the only
everlasting matter in the world. We have an everlasting
message committed to us concerning 'a lamb without
blemish and without spot: who verily was foreordained
before the foundation of the world'. We have 'the everlasting gospel' to preach (Rev. 14:6).

Sin has so blinded man that he believes in the eternity of matter, but not in the eternity of God's message to this world. Man argues, 'What are mere words beside the realities of this present world?' Our words are not enough to answer him. We must let Christ speak to him in his blindness and remind him, 'Heaven and earth shall pass away; but my words shall not pass away' (Mark 13:31). The problem of man ignoring the importance of the gospel message, beside the apparent permanence of man and his achievements, is not a new one, for it also faced the New Testament church. Peter felt it to be a matter of such importance that he wrote a letter about it, in which he declared, 'For all flesh is as grass, and all the glory of man as the flower of grass. The grass withereth and the flower thereof falleth away: but the word of the Lord endureth for ever. And this is the word which by the gospel is preached unto you' (1 Peter 1: 24-25).

The two persons walking along the Emmaus road should never have been taken by surprise by the fact and reality of the resurrection. God had indeed been preparing the world for this momentous event for a few thousand years. No doubt Christ traced the thread of hope running through the ancient world, for in the Bible there is a growing and progressive view of the coming of the risen Lord. Surely, He would have reminded these people of Abraham, who rises like a peak of faith towering above the men of his day. The only thing that succoured Him in his greatest trial of faith, when it seemed certain that he would have to sacrifice his own son to God, was his belief in the resurrection, 'accounting that God was able to raise him up, even from the dead; from whence also he received him in a figure' (Heb. 11:19). Here is a picture of an early believer, without the help of the written Gospels and the Epistles with their developed doctrine of the resurrection, rising to unparalleled heights of faith.

## The hope of the resurrection

In every age before the incarnation of Christ, and especially in times of tremendous trial and human hopelessness, God inspired some men to believe in the hope of the resurrection. When people were often hard-pressed and in great and seemingly unbearable suffering, their faith rose to the heights of the risen Lord. Job was such a man. Totally disillusioned by the so-called comforters of his day, deserted by his wife, desolated by the death of his ten children in one day, and diseased in body, he wanted to leave behind him the secret of his being able, not merely to cope with his domestic situation, but to triumph in it. He called for an iron pen to leave the record graven in the rock for ever. He longed that a biography be written of his life — and God obliged most wonderfully! (Job 19: 23,24.) The secret source of his faith cried out, 'For I know that my redeemer liveth, and that He shall stand at the latter day upon the earth: and though after my skin worms destroy this body, yet in my flesh shall I see God' (Job 19: 25,26).

Christ may well have gone on to rebuke the two travellers on the Emmaus road for their forgetfulness of Daniel who, when God's people were undergoing the long exile of seventy years in a foreign land, was enabled by faith to see that justice would be vindicated at the resurrection of all mankind and the ensuing judgement when 'many of them that sleep in the dust of the earth shall awake, some to everlasting life, and some to shame and everlasting contempt' (Dan. 12:2).

Above all else, surely, Christ must have recalled David's immortal words, which were later shown by Peter to be Christ's own words of hope and triumph over death: 'For thou wilt not leave my soul in hell [Sheol]; neither wilt thou suffer thine Holy One to see corruption' (Ps. 16:10; Acts 2:23-27). Such passages, and many others, were no doubt used by Christ to administer this rebuke in the face of the surprise and unbelief at His own resurrection appearance. As we have already seen, the early news of Christ's resurrection was received as 'idle tales and they believed them not', for the history of the world is largely a history of man's unbelief.

We live in a day which either doubts or denies one of

the cardinal truths of Christianity, namely, the resurrection, the fact that the Son of God, who died for our sins, rose again triumphant the third day, leaving behind Him not only an empty cross but an empty tomb. Dying as a man, He rose as a man. A body was crucified and a body was resurrected. But in our day there is a growing rejection of the fact of the physical resurrection of Christ, and therefore of the future physical resurrection of man.

The faith of some people today is being undermined because certain men in high positions and, alas, even some ministers are openly denying the truth of the resurrection. It is regarded as an insult to the intelligence of a man living in a nuclear age. Some people would maintain that scientific advancements have disproved the resurrection, and so modern man must think again.

It seems to me that one of the basic failures of our age is that man living in the twentieth century believes that he is the first to deny the resurrection. But the resurrection of Christ has always been either rejected or accepted. However, one point needs to be made plain. The early church would not have dared to call itself Christian and yet at the same time to deny the resurrection. To them the resurrection of Christ was the cardinal doctrine linked with the death of Christ on the cross. In fact, without the resurrection there clearly was no message for the church to preach. And that is not too dogmatic a statement. After the death of Judas, when the other apostles considered the qualifications of an apostle to be appointed in his place, they knew one essential truth that God required of him. He 'must . . . be ordained to be a witness with us of His resurrection' (Acts 1:22). We should not be surprised therefore to find the apostle Paul preaching this truth in Greece. What would surprise some people today is that he preached it to the most intellectual and sophisticated people in the world. He even dared to go to Mars' Hill where the philosophical set met (see Acts 17). Now I believe this is what we must not be afraid to do today. The point I want to make is that though Paul knew the modern man's attitude to the resurrection he still preached the resurrection! This is no doubt a word in season for many who feel that we must leave out today those truths which are likely to cause offence. Yet when we follow through Paul's sermon we find a definite development of thought. He revealed that his faith rested in a God whom he knew and worshipped, whereas they worshipped an unknown god. He showed them that the God who created the world is governing the world, even in fact determining the duration of man's life, and the places where he should live. Now twentieth-century man probably would say that was sufficient. Anyone who believes that is a Christian. But Paul knew that was not enough. He made plain that 'God commandeth all men everywhere to repent'. For he knew that men everywhere have sinned against God. And has not the God against whom they have sinned a right to command the sinner to repent? For, we may be sure, God has appointed a day in which He will judge the world by the man He has appointed. Yet the message Paul preached concluded that God 'hath given assurance [or better, a guarantee] unto all men, in that he hath raised him from the dead' (Acts 17:31). God assures us now that the Judge is alive. And the Scripture makes abundantly plain that the next great event after our physical resurrection will be our judgement (Heb. 9:27). This may seem an impossible event to twentieth-century man, but Christ tells him, 'Marvel not at this: for the hour is coming, in the which all that are in the graves shall hear His voice' (John 5:28).

## The greatest harvest in the world

Christ further taught that His death and resurrection would produce the greatest harvest in the world. To those who really want to find Christ in the twentieth century, He still gives His first answer: 'Verily, verily, I say unto you, Except a corn of wheat fall into the ground and die, it abideth alone: but if it die, it bringeth forth much fruit' (John 12:24).

The way of death is the way to life. The law of nature is that in seeds and plants life comes by death. The seed must be put into the ground and must decay and die if we want it to bear fruit and produce a harvest. This beautiful figure is used by the Lord Jesus Christ, the Lord of the harvest, to unfold an even greater truth, that this is also the law of salvation. He must die before we can live. His death is the only way to bring spiritual life to man. The world expected to see Christ reign as a king, but instead they saw Him die a slave's death in great shame and humiliation. For as Bishop Ryle profoundly states, 'He came to carry a cross and not to wear a crown. . . . The kingdom He came to set up was to begin with a crucifixion, and not with a coronation.'

Study Christ in the Gospels and you will see that it was not from His life but from His death that there came forth a great harvest of souls. It was not the power of His preaching, nor that of His miracles, but the power which flowed from His death and resurrection which has made such a great change in the lives of men.

His death was to be the source of spiritual life to millions from every nation and of every language. But the death was absolutely necessary for the fruit to come. As Christ Himself said, 'Except a corn of wheat fall into the ground and die, it abideth alone.' Matthew Henry observes that the seed fell to the ground in the incarnation, but it did not bring forth fruit until Christ died. If He had not died for our sins, we are left in no doubt of what the consequences would have been. He would have remained alone. There would have been only one man in heaven. Thanks be to God, that is not true. Christ, the heavenly grain of wheat, did die. But there is an even more wonderful truth: 'But now is Christ risen from the dead, and become the firstfruits of them that slept' (1 Cor. 15:20). Christ has risen triumphant for Christians of all ages. Christ's resurrection was the first sheaf of the great harvest to come. All who truly believe that He died for their sins may also know that spiritually speaking they are now 'risen with Christ' (Col. 3:1). Yet the final great harvest is to come when Christ shall return and 'the dead shall be raised incorruptible'. We who have trusted in Christ as our Saviour can say today, 'O death, where is thy sting? O grave where is thy victory?'

and we can conclude by saying, 'But thanks be to God which giveth us the victory through our Lord Jesus Christ.'

The harvest is certain, for Isaiah of old could say, 'When thou shalt make His soul an offering for sin he shall see his seed.' Christ knew that His death would not be in vain. He knew that, 'If it die, it bringeth forth much fruit.' How wonderful to know that there is a day coming when the harvest of souls will be gathered in and 'he *shall* see his seed', and again, 'he *shall* see of the travail of his soul, and shall be satisfied'. May no one reading this book have to conclude, 'The harvest is past, the summer is ended, and we are not saved.'

## Miracle or myth?

Finally, as we are still confronted with a world which asks whether the resurrection is miracle or myth, fact or fiction, we must again return to that way of preaching this God-given gospel used by the apostle Paul. There is no greater summary of gospel preaching in general, and preaching the resurrection in particular, than that found in 1 Corinthians 15: 1-22. This is a kind of documentary evidence for the gospel of God.

Paul begins by stating that Christianity is God's declaration to man. It is not man's ideas about God. The declaration is communicated by the preaching of the gospel. He recalls to their mind 'the gospel which I preached unto you'. Yet there was also the personal reception of that gospel. It has clearly become the platform, the rock, the foundation of their lives, for he can assure them it is the gospel 'wherein ye stand'. A God-given gospel preacher must exhort his hearers, 'Keep in memory what I preached unto you.' There must be the retention of the gospel. The alternative is a fearful possibility of a false belief: 'Unless ye have believed in vain.' Paul shows that the gospel must be received by the preacher before he passes it on to his congregation. Paul delivered what he 'first believed'. Preaching is delivering what man has first received from God. It is accompanied by the God-given authority for the death and resurrection of Christ: He 'died for our sins . . . he was buried . . . he rose again the third day'. Yet here is the genius of gospel preaching. Its authority is not derived from the ability of the preacher, but is 'according to the scriptures'. We must tell the world that the evidence for the death and resurrection of Christ does not rest on questionable hearsay evidence, passed down over two thousand years, but rather upon the Scriptures which are God's sacred writings. These declare the death of God the Son for our sins as our only way of deliverance from those sins by His physical resurrection from the dead. The whole power of the gospel is that the Christ it describes was dead, but now is alive again for evermore, whereas every other religion is a dead religion, possessing a prophet who either will die or has already died. Paul unashamedly revealed the visible authority for the resurrection of Christ six times in a row! He was *seen* 'of Cephas'; *seen* 'then of the twelve'; *seen* 'of above five hundred' at once, the majority of whom were still alive and clearly could be called up as eye-witnesses; *seen* 'of James'; *seen* 'then of all the apostles'; *seen* 'of me also', that is, *seen* last of all by the writer himself.

Paul then shows that a sight of the risen Lord through scriptural preaching is both a humbling and transforming experience. He attributes his changed life solely to the grace of God. Though the least of the apostles in his own estimation, he has accomplished the most for God in his labouring exploits. The resurrection for Paul was an unashamedly divisive truth: some 'believed' while others retorted, 'There is no resurrection from the dead.' Yet Paul's preaching was not silenced by godless denial of the resurrection. He confronted the doubters immediately with the consequences of no resurrection, describing a logical landslide to misery. The consequences follow hard on the heels of one another. If Christ is not risen, the content of preaching is a lie, faith is worthless, resting on a falsehood. We are witnessing something which never happened. The dead are dead, the professing believer is still in sin and the dead believers have perished. The believer is left as the most miserable man in the world. For a hope in Christ in this life only makes a

man of 'all men most miserable'. For the misery of a world
without Christianity, without the risen Lord, is the misery
of a world which is perishing without future life and hope.
Take away the risen Lord, and you take away God, salvation, resurrection, life, hope and heaven ahead. But,
thank God, 'now is Christ risen from the dead' as the 'firstfruits of them that slept'. As man was the bringer of death,
so Man also is the bringer of life from the dead: 'By man
came death, by man came also the resurrection of the dead.'
As the first man, Adam, was the bringer of universal death,
so in Christ there is the only power in the world to make
man alive unto God for ever: 'For as in Adam all die, even
so in Christ shall all be made alive.' Clearly the preaching of a
God-given gospel is not merely a matter of opinion, but a
matter of life and death.


1. See Tacitus: *Annals* XV:44
2. Suetonius: *Claudius,* XXV
3. Pliny: *Epis* XCVII

# 2
# God-given agency

God in His provision for the evangelization of His world has given us an agency of evangelism. The whole question here is: 'To whom did Christ commit the gospel before He left the world and physically ascended to heaven?' For the answer, we need to look at the familiar and yet wonderful commission of Christ to the church (Matt. 28:18-20). We are well aware that it was given originally to the apostles, but Christ clearly intended it to be passed on to the church of all generations: 'And Jesus came and spake unto them, saying, All power is given unto me in heaven and in earth. Go ye therefore, and teach all nations, baptizing them in the name of the Father, and of the Son, and of the Holy Ghost: teaching them to observe all things whatsoever I have commanded you: and, lo, I am with you alway, even unto the end of the world.'

## Unfulfilled commission

Here we have before us, firstly, the challenge of an unfulfilled commission to the church. We do not for a moment suggest that the apostles did not fulfil their part, but the real question is: 'Have we fulfilled ours?' We still have an *unfulfilled* commission to the church of God to take the gospel to every creature (Mark 16:15). It is unfulfilled because it is to all nations and to every creature. We have therefore a continuing commission to the church today. Secondly, we have received *from Christ* a *lasting* commission to evangelize. For it is unto 'the end of the world' or, literally, 'unto the end of the ages'.

To these words might be added the last recorded words of Christ on earth: 'the uttermost part of the earth' (Acts 1:8). The last words of any man are worth listening to, but never were more important last words ever spoken than these. But they seem largely to have been forgotten by man, in that he has done so little for the accomplishment of that great end of evangelizing the whole world.

Indeed, shortly before His crucifixion, Christ spoke of the end of the world. He did not dwell upon atomic, hydrogen or neutron bombs as the sign of the end, though He did promise the sad continuance of wars and rumours of wars. No, He foretold the sign of the end of this world in these dramatic words: 'And this gospel of the kingdom shall be preached in all the world for a witness unto all nations; and then shall the end come' (Matt. 24:14). Let us therefore with gratitude learn that God is not leaving the destiny of the world to be determined by the deliberations of left or right-wing politicians, nor by the utopian dreams of evolutionists, but by the preaching of the gospel.

### Gift of evangelist

How has God equipped His church to carry out this momentous task? We look no further than the New Testament to see that God has given a very special gift to His church — the gift of evangelists. Only three times do we find this wonderful gift described. The first is in Ephesians 4:11: 'And he gave some, . . . evangelists . . .' In Acts 21:8 we have an equally brief mention, where we read, '. . . Philip the evangelist . . .'. We may well ask, how did these evangelists evangelize? In the eighth chapter of the Acts of the Apostles we are given the privilege of observing a New Testament evangelist in action, Philip by name. We catch him in the act of preaching: 'Then Philip went down to the city of Samaria, and preached Christ unto them' (Acts 8:5). This describes the kingly high calling of an evangelist, in the sense that the word preached conveys the idea of 'heralding'. Incidentally, at least sixty times in the New Testament, the preacher is seen as an ambassador for Christ, heralding forth the message of the King of kings to a lost world.

Philip was an effective evangelist; effective not in the use of some modern methods of communication or gimmicks of his day, but by the sheer authority of his God-given message. This made the people not only stop what they were doing, but listen and believe! It was the message, not the evangelist himself, that mattered to them. For we read, 'And the people with one accord gave heed unto those things which Philip spake . . .' (v.6). In a later chapter, we shall develop the idea of Philip as an evangelist directed by God, as we trace the movement of this desert mission (vv.26,29). As we observe Philip, we are immediately challenged by the earnestness of his ministry. The task gripped him as much as the people to whom he spoke. He literally ran to evangelize, so certain was he that he was sent by God: 'Philip ran thither to him' (v.29). There was earnestness, fervour and a sense of urgency to take the gospel to the Ethiopian in his great need.

In this one man we find both a mass evangelist and a personal evangelist. One day we see him preaching to Samaria and, as it were, the next to this lone man in the midst of a desert, the Chancellor of the Exchequer of the Queen of the Ethiopians. In this he resembled his Lord, who was equally at home preaching to the multitudes or, to the highly moral 'archbishop' of the Jews, Nicodemus, or, practically the next moment, to the immoral woman by the well (see John chapters 3 and 4). So often we envy the fruit of Peter's ministry at Pentecost in the three thousand souls saved, but forget the lesson he had to learn that the solitary soul of Cornelius equally mattered to God (see Acts 2 and 10). In the twentieth century we have often made a false distinction between the mass evangelist and the personal worker, yet such a distinction was unknown in the times of Christ and the apostles.

Finally, Philip was an itinerant evangelist, for this vital chapter, showing us the fiery evangelist of God, closes with a description of the scope and area of his work and records, 'And passing through he preached in all the cities, till he came to Caesarea' (Acts 8:40).

In following the ministry of a New Testament evangelist, we shall see how his ministry differed from that of a pastor and teacher (Eph. 4:11). An evangelist, though preaching the same gospel of redemption, was preaching to the unconverted and not to Christians. Nor was he resident in one place overseeing a settled congregation of believers, but rather, from the basis of the nearest local church, he launched out into the unevangelized areas where at present no church existed and where, in most cases, not one Christian was to be found for miles around.

We urgently need today to look for such men as Philip in our churches — men who are gifted by God to be pioneer evangelists in the unevangelized regions beyond the churches. However, even in New Testament times, when an evangelist was not present in the congregation the apostles clearly had authority to call upon a minister to 'do the work of an evangelist'. Timothy was called upon in this way by Paul. Timothy was probably a 'mission convert' from Paul's first evangelistic outreach and later accompanied him on further missions to the lost. No doubt it was on these occasions that Paul discovered the evangelistic gift in him. This should challenge us in our day that no pastor is exempt from a responsibility to evangelize lost men and women outside the scope of his church on account of his primary teaching and pastoral responsibilities. Clearly a pastor in New Testament times had to be flexible, and ready to respond to the spontaneous call to 'do the work of an evangelist'.

We find, then, an apostle giving a charge to a minister also to 'do the work of an evangelist, make full proof of (or fulfil) thy ministry' (2 Tim. 4:5). It is taken for granted, not only that Timothy knows that evangelists still exist in this later period in the history of the church, but that he understands what an evangelist is, for no definition as such is specifically given. Rather he is told how to evangelize. Let us therefore look at this apostolic charge to do the work of an evangelist.

The first point we notice is that the evangelist is to carry out his task in the sight of God. He is to be more conscious of God than even of the people to whom he preaches. The charge that fell upon Timothy's ears was this: 'I charge thee therefore before God, and the Lord Jesus Christ . . .' (2 Tim. 4:1).

Firstly, God comes before man in evangelism, and secondly, eternity comes before time, or judgement before salvation, for the charge continues, 'Who shall judge the quick and the dead at his appearing and his kingdom.' What a fearful thought! Before we reach for our sermon notes and our Bible and pack our bags for the next mission, we must stop and listen to this awful charge. We must look at both the beginning and end of our evangelism. We must start with God and end with God in judgement, for God will judge both the evangelist and the evangelized in the Day of Judgement. Let us remember that the next souls to whom we preach the gospel will be judged by what we say to them!

Thirdly, the evangelist is to evangelize at all times, for he is commanded (there is no option!): 'Preach the Word; be instant in season, out of season' (v.2). No time is inopportune to preach the gospel.

Fourthly, a convicting gospel must be preached. The evangelist is not a comedian, or entertainer, but one who convicts. Great seriousness is required, in both the matter and the manner in which the gospel is presented, for he is called to 'reprove, rebuke, exhort with all long-suffering' (v.2).

Fifthly, a doctrinal gospel must be preached. For the evangelist's message must have doctrinal content concerning God, man and sin, heaven and hell. Paul concludes with the important words: 'and doctrine'. For too long, alas, generally speaking, the twentieth-century church has given the impression that it regards the evangelist (when it believes in his existence) as someone who is inferior to a pastor and teacher. He has a different office, but he has the same gospel to preach. Evangelistic preaching has too often been caricatured as a mere recitation of texts beginning and ending with John 3:16, punctuated with appeals, more often from the evangelist than from Scripture. Clearly in the light of this commission to Timothy, the evangelist should have as deep a knowledge of the great doctrines of the faith as any other minister of the gospel. This fact can surely be proved by examining the evangelical sermons of men of biblical and more recent times, such as Paul and George Whitefield.

It is vital also to notice the reason why the apostle Paul especially called upon the evangelist Timothy to preach doctrinal sermons. It was in the light of the forthcoming apostasy, when men would not endure sound doctrine — 'sound' in the sense of 'imparting health'. It is interesting that the Greek word used is the one which we use for hygiene in everyday language. The spiritual health of a nation therefore depends upon the preaching of the healthy words of the living God. Paul also warned Timothy that such doctrinal preaching would not be popular, since the personal preference of the people would be for a more appealing type of ministry, which would aim at pleasing the taste of the hearers and would be composed of man's fables rather than God's facts. We may therefore take heart in the knowledge that even in apostolic times the popular evangelist, who tickled the ear of the people, had arrived. Let us also learn that God commands living, dynamic, doctrinal preaching as the only answer to man's deepest needs. It is always God, the divine dietician, who must decide the food the preacher is to give the people — not man himself.

Sixthly, and finally, in our study of a New Testament evangelist, we see that the evangelist Timothy was to continue the evangelizing ministry of the apostle Paul. We do not believe in an apostolic succession, but we do believe we have the apostles' doctrine handed down to us, as Paul instructed Timothy that 'the things that thou hast heard of me among many witnesses, the same commit thou to faithful men, who shall be able to teach others also' (2 Tim. 2:2).

### Spiritual sunbeams

It is wonderful to read in the early history of the church

how that was exactly what did happen. The early church historian Eusebius informs us 'how that in short space the gospel was published throughout the world'. He tells us plainly and graphically how this was done: 'With the divine co-operation, the doctrine of the Saviour, like the rays of the sun, quickly illumined the whole world; and straight-way, in accordance with the divine Scriptures, the voice of the inspired evangelists and apostles went forth through all the earth, and their words to the end of the world. In every city and village, churches were quickly established, filled with multitudes of people like a replenished threshing-floor. And those whose minds, in consequence of errors which had descended to them from their forefathers, were fettered by the ancient disease of idolatrous superstition, were, by the power of Christ operating through the teaching and the wonderful works of his disciples, set free, as it were, from terrible masters, and found a release from the most cruel bondage. They renounced with abhorrence every species of demoniacal polytheism, and confessed that there was only one God, the creator of all things, and him they honoured with the rites of true piety, through the inspired and rational worship which has been planted by our Saviour among men.'[1]

Eusebius takes us beyond New Testament times in his account of the early evangelists. He tells us how 'those occupying the first steps in succession from the apostles set out on journeys from home to perform the work of evangelists and to preach to such as had not heard the word of faith'. He speaks of one called Pantanus of Alexandria as one of many evangelists of the Word, after the manner of the apostles. He mentions Mark as the first preacher to the Egyptians, and the early entry of the gospel into Ethiopia. He sums up wonderfully the early evangelization of the world in these heart-stirring words: 'The divine and admirable disciples of the apostles built up the superstruc-ture of the churches, the foundation whereof the apostles had laid in all places where they came. They everywhere promoted the preaching of the gospel, sowing the seeds of heavenly doctrine through the whole world. Many of the

disciples then alive distributed their estates to the poor,
and leaving their own country, did the work of evangelists
to those who had never heard the Christian faith; preaching Christ and delivering the evangelical writings to them.
No sooner had they planted the faith in any foreign countries and ordained guides and pastors to whom they committed the care of their new plantations, than they went to
the nations, assisted by the grace and powerful working of
the Holy Spirit. As soon as they began to preach the gospel,
the people flocked to them and cheerfully worshipped the
true God, piously and heartily believing in His Name.'

May we be given again this vision of those early evangelists, whose preaching not only converted souls, but
created churches, and who did not feel that they had completed their work until pastors had been appointed. Only
then did they move on to another unevangelized field and
begin again.


## The morning star

Sadly, however, we lose sight of these amazing evangelists,
these sunbeams of God, in the long night of the Dark Ages,
lightened only momentarily by the heroic faith of the
Albigenses and Waldenses, who lie outside the scope of this
book. We have to look further, however, if we would find
again a man who not only believed in the God-given gift of
evangelists to His church, but who actually trained them
and thrust them forth into the length and breadth of the
land. That land was Britain and that man was John Wycliffe,
rightly called the 'Morning Star of the Reformation'. God
raised him up in the fourteenth century, not only, we
believe, to translate the Bible into the common language of
the people, but also to train evangelists to preach the
gospel in the same common language. Though we cannot
put our finger upon that momentous moment of history
when he began to do this, it is highly possible that even
while a Doctor of Divinity at Oxford University he drew
around him young men of God, to whom he communicated
his burning zeal and vision for the evangelization of Britain.

Whether this work began then, or later in his rural parish of Lutterworth, ultimately is not important. What matters is that he did it and God honoured him in the doing. Vaughan, one of his biographers, writes, 'Both by word and deed he laboured to promote everywhere the right preaching of the gospel and the most effective instrumentality which he used for that end was the institution of a preaching itinerancy.' This evangelistic movement had inevitably to be achieved without any recognized church authority and basis. Yet so effective was it under the hand of God that Courtney, the archbishop of the day, was forced, though no doubt reluctantly, to acknowledge its country-wide influence. In his *Mandate to the Bishop of London* he speaks of 'certain unauthorized itinerant preachers who,' as he had unhappily been compelled to learn, 'set forth erroneous — yea heretical — assertions in public sermons, not only in public squares and other profane places' and 'they do this' he adds, with special emphasis, 'under the guise of true holiness but without having obtained any episcopal or papal authorization'. The date of this mandate shows that the evangelization was in full swing by May 1382. These 'evangelical men' or 'apostolic men' as Wycliffe came affectionately to describe them, became a familiar sight in the land, dressed in the clothes of the day, consisting of long coarse red woollen garments, staff in hand, and without shoes of any kind. Yet the 'beautiful feet' of these fourteenth-century evangelists carried them from village to village and town to town 'without halt or rest', from Norwich to Llandaff, preaching the gospel wherever people were willing to listen, in the church when the door was open to them, or else in any street or market-place in the land. Their chief duty, in the view of Lechler, was the 'faithful scattering of the seed of God's Word'. It was Wycliffe's declared aim by both his preaching and writings 'to lead back the church to the ordinance of Christ and pure conformity to His Word'.

We have reason to believe that some of the writings of Wycliffe found their way across the sea into the continent of Europe and were the means of the conversion of John

Huss, who became a veritable John the Baptist, a flaming evangelist preaching the gospel across Bohemia, and whose ministry could only be halted by his being placed in the stocks by day and tortured on the rack at night, until he died a martyr's death at the stake in 1415.

For a time even after the death of Wycliffe in 1384, the itinerant preachers or evangelists continued to thrive in the form of the Lollards, a name of uncertain origin but used to describe the followers of Wycliffe.

The impact of the preaching of Wycliffe's 'evangelical men' in conversions is almost beyond description. The antagonistic chronicler of Leicester, Knighton, was forced to admit, 'You could not meet two persons in the highway but one of them was Wycliffe's disciple.' Therefore the claim that half the population of the country was on the side of the Lollards was not unfounded, and these men clearly studied, adopted and preached these evangelical principles.

Let us catch one of Wycliffe's, or rather God's, fourteenth-century evangelists in action. William Swinderby, a converted priest, had been set apart by Wycliffe as an itinerant preacher. His evangelical preaching spoke powerfully to the times and to the sins of church and people. His frugal and solitary way of life led him to be known as 'William the Hermit'. His fearless preaching, condemning the affluence of society, made the Catholic chronicler Knighton confess that 'some honest men were well-nigh driven to despair'. Yet when the doors of the church and gates of the churchyard were shut against Swinderby, the preacher constructed his own pulpit out of two millstones in the High Street of Leicester and preached despite the opposition of the bishop. We are again indebted to Knighton for informing us of the impact of such preaching. He says, 'You might see throngs of people from every part, as well from the town as the country, double the number there used to be when they might hear him lawfully.' We have reason to believe, though records are not abundant, that rich and poor flocked to hear and to heed the claims of Christ upon their lives, and joined the ranks of the Lollards.

The sole purpose of this brief historical and biographical account is to show that where men have believed in, recognized and trained evangelists, the life of the nation, and in some degree of the church, has been radically changed. As we leave this period of history we see that, following the ministry of Wycliffe and his evangelists, the gospel had reached into Eastern England to Norwich, down southward to London, across to Salisbury and westward into Wales.

Again we largely lose sight of the evangelist in the history of the church as we enter those dark days heralding the great period of the Reformation. Though we have no real evidence that the training and thrusting forth of evangelists continued beyond Wycliffe and the Lollards, we must believe that it was because of the state of the church that Wycliffe was forced to work not only outside, but against, the professing church of the day. Evangelists therefore could not be sent forth from the local evangelical churches of the day because these did not exist. In a sense, sad though it is to relate, the burden, vision and need for evangelists died with Wycliffe, whose 'star' waned and whose influence for nearly a century was felt no more.

## Forgotten gift

Indeed it has been truly said, 'Prior to the Reformation, preaching had fallen into such neglect that it had virtually ceased to be a function of the church.' The Reformers of the sixteenth century reintroduced both the Word of God as the authority of the church and preaching as the vehicle whereby that Word of God should again reach the people of England. Yet even with great preachers such as Bilney and Latimer, strange though it may seem, the Reformers' theology of evangelism largely 'removed' the office of New Testament evangelist from the church of the succeeding centuries. The view of the Reformers generally was that the gift of evangelists ceased at the end of the apostolic period with the founding of the church. In their exposition of Ephesians 4:11 they coupled the gift of evangelists with those of apostles and prophets as extraordinary gifts. For them the evangelists were essentially in New Testament times apostolic delegates or representatives. We have no battle with them over the uniqueness of the ministry of New Testament apostles and prophets as extraordinary gifts to lay the foundation of the church once and for ever. We also acknowledge, as we have already seen, that Timothy received an apostolic charge to do 'the work of an evangelist'.

We would ask, however, if the gift of evangelists is merely a foundational gift to the church, to be placed side by side with apostles and prophets, then why did the apostle Paul omit to mention them in Ephesians 2:20 where we read, 'And are built upon the foundation of the apostles and prophets . . .'? Surely we would expect the evangelist to be found here to substantiate the case. We would also strongly question whether Scripture warrants our defining the primary role of an evangelist as an apostolic delegate or representative. We know, on the contrary, that the meaning of 'evangelist' is rather a preacher of the gospel. We submit that the Reformers' removal of the New Testament gift of evangelist from church order has not only cast a cloud over the church's subsequent understanding of the office, but has biased the church towards a historical interpretation rather than a primarily biblical one, in that most recognized commentators upon Ephesians 4:11 are largely governed by the interpretation of the Reformers and give only a small place to the alternative view of the evangelist as an itinerant preacher.

In the seventeenth century Philip Doddridge describes evangelists as those 'who were to travel from place to place and were to fulfil such particular commission as the apostles should give in settling and establishing churches they had planted'. If one comes right up to date and picks up commentaries of the present time, the evangelists are described as 'of lower rank than the apostles under whom they worked' or again, 'We may assume that theirs was an itinerant work of preaching under the apostles and it may be fair to call them the rank and file missionaries of the church.' Too long we have raised our eyebrows and our voices against the modern evangelist who in our esteem has been often self-appointed, and who has embarked on his crusades outside the church's control. Is not this the logical outcome of the Reformed church's disbelief in the existence of New Testament evangelists working from and with the local church?

Yet, strange though it may seem, John Calvin, though on the one hand he taught in his *Institutes of the Christian Religion,* 'God adorned His church with apostles, evangelists and prophets only for a time', on the other, he goes on to say, 'except where religion has broken down, He raises up evangelists apart from church order to restore pure doctrine to its lost position.'

## Mastermind

John Calvin himself masterminded a great evangelistic mission to France. In 1555 the evangelization of France from Geneva really began. In all some eighty-eight men were sent to evangelize France. Nothing is known of the social background of forty-six of these men, but we find that the remaining forty-two were drawn from a cross-section of noble, bourgeois and artisan backgrounds. It is interesting to notice that not one came from a peasant background, though sixteenth century society seems to have contained a high proportion of peasants. The nationality of these pastors doing the 'work of an evangelist' was nearly always French. They caught their evangelistic fire and vision at Geneva and they returned to evangelize the country from which they had originally fled because of persecution. Twenty-nine of those who came to Geneva had already held pastorates in France, but in Geneva they underwent training to be missionary-pastors.

Originally training was available at Lausanne as well as Geneva, but in 1550 the pastors responsible for training in the Academy fell out of favour with the Berne Government and were expelled, so from then onward the training centre on Geneva alone. Many flocked from the Lausanne area to Geneva. Here the students hung on the words of

John Calvin as he laboured to expound the Scriptures line
by line, not moving from one book of the Bible to another
until he had thoroughly exhausted its contents. Geneva
was in every sense a city of Bible students. It must have
been an amazing sight to see a thousand students a day sitting at the feet of Calvin and, more importantly, at the
feet of Almighty God. Calvin was, of course, assisted by
that great bearded wonder of evangelistic fire and vision,
William Farel. It is fascinating 'to look over the shoulder'
of one of these missionary students in preparation for his
life and work as he burnt the midnight oil over Luther's
commentary on Galatians, Calvin on Isaiah or Romans, or
Erasmus on the Gospel of John. This was the 'food' on
which the evangelists were fed before being thrust forth
into the needy field of France. Some of these men were
married, but like soldiers going forth to war they left their
wives behind. We are told, however, that the wives still
received their husbands' stipends in their absence. The
single students were often billeted out in the homes of
their professors, no doubt being moulded by the wisdom,
experience and godly characters of such great men of God.
The financial support of these missionaries was generally
borne by their own congregations back in France. Yet
sixteenth-century students were no different from their
twentieth-century counterparts in taking jobs to put themselves through college. Some took posts as tutors and some
even as secretaries to ministers!

These students were not sent out as missionary pastors/
evangelists until after several years of close supervision by
the Geneva Company of Pastors. In every city there was a
company of pastors or *Classe* responsible to the city government for filling pastoral vacancies in the city and in the
adjoining villages. These students were not immediately
sent back to France, but often served first in French
Switzerland. During the years 1555-62 but especially in
1558 and 1559, these eighty-eight men were thrust forth
to accomplish the evangelization of France, and between
them they took up a hundred and five appointments. That
such men had to be preachers we are left in no doubt, for

they had to give an oral exposition of a selected text. Those whose voices were not loud enough, or whose manner was too timid for missionaries, were either turned down or sent as teachers to village appointments.

The Geneva School of Pastors generally sent their pastors in response to requests in letters, sometimes addressed to Calvin personally. The appointments considered not only the ability of the missionary, but the needy areas of France. These fearless evangelists had to be smuggled into France, undertaking perilous journeys along lonely mountain trails. Calvin's evangelistic mission depended on his missionaries remaining incognito six days of the week and then preaching in a house or secret place on the Lord's Day. If a pastor was found out he was very likely to lose his life, such was the hatred for these sixteenth-century evangelists. Therefore great secrecy was adopted in the methods used. Meetings were generally held in the private homes of members of the church at night. Each member was searched on arrival. Others met in barns, woods or in fields to declare and listen to the wonderful gospel. At Castres Geoffrey Brun was despatched from Geneva to begin his evangelistic ministry in 1560. Beginning in a private home, the work grew so much, even under persecution, that he had to move to another home of a Christian believer. An assistant minister had to be appointed and in time public buildings had to be rented for the preaching of the gospel, when the congregation outgrew the private homes of believers. This work was finally hindered in the time of the religious wars. Our evidence of the extent of this evangelization of France is based on a request of Queen Regent Catherine de Medici early in 1562, which revealed some 2,150 churches of the Huguenots with a membership of 3,000,000 out of a population estimated by the historian Doumergue at 20,000,000.

The work clearly declined as Calvin declined in health, for between 1563 and 1572 only thirty-one men were sent out to evangelize France — few in comparison with the previous years. A final factor was the plague which affected Geneva particularly in 1564 and 1568-70, causing a reduction in the number of students.

## Gift for today?

We dare not leave this Reformation period without noting
that Martin Luther himself clearly saw it as a time of great
evangelization of the Continent of Europe. He equated
Reformation and evangelism, declaring, 'If I should want
to boast, I should glory in God that I am one of the apostles
and evangelists in German lands, even though the devil
and all his bishops and tyrants do not want me to be such:
for I know that by the grace of God I taught and still teach
faith and truth.' He also calls himself 'an unworthy evangelist of our Lord Jesus Christ'.

Was there ever a day when we should expect to see God's
gift of evangelist to the church of God acknowledged and
operative in the churches? To be fair, R. B. Kuiper, writing
in this present century, upholds a similar view to the
Reformers, but he does add, 'True, at present, the church
has no longer evangelists in the specific and special sense
which was in vogue in the apostolic church. But this is not
a compelling reason for the avoidance of the name.'

What is equally significant is that we have seen from
Eusebius that the disciples of the apostles continued to
function as evangelists, both as the instruments of saving
souls and of establishing new local churches in foreign lands.
Though they clearly believed that the foundational truths
were given once and for all, they saw that throughout the
then world there was a place for evangelists in order to
see more and more souls saved and churches established.
The early history of the church therefore supports the fact
that evangelists did continue after the apostles. Again,
returning to the idea of the evangelist as an apostolic
delegate, no one seems able to fit the evangelist Philip into
that interpretative mould. We have also seen earlier how, in
pre-Reformation times, John Wycliffe and his evangelists
were honoured by God to bring about at least the nominal
conversion of half of England.

Perhaps the greatest question we are left with is this:
'Would Christ have commissioned His church to evangelize
His lost world to the end of time and then immediately
remove the greatest gift for accomplishing that great end,

namely, the evangelist?' Surely that is an unthinkable and unbiblical conclusion.

## The unchained evangelist

Certainly in the seventeenth century, the time of the Puritans, there was at least one great man who believed in evangelists — namely, John Bunyan. In *Pilgrim's Progress,* we have this delightful description of an evangelist: 'a man who had his eyes up to heaven, the best of books was in his hand, the law of truth was written upon his lips and he stood as if he pleaded with me'. Later, when Christian came into the house of the Interpreter, he was shown a picture of the evangelist: 'The man whose picture this is', said the Interpreter, 'is one of a thousand . . . I have showed thee this picture first, because the man whose picture this is, is the only man whom the Lord of the place whither thou art going, hath authorized to be thy guide.'

In fact, John Bunyan gives us an account of his call to minister not only to the converted, but to the unevangelized masses of the land.[2] He informs us, 'I was more particularly called forth and appointed to a more ordinary and public preaching of the word, not only to and among them that believed, but also to offer the gospel to those who had not yet received the faith thereof: about which time I did evidently find in my mind a secret inclination thereto.' He was honoured in a most immediate and remarkable way when he began to preach. For he tells us, 'When the country understood, they came to hear the word by hundreds, and that from all parts, though upon divers and sundry accounts.' Bunyan, like his dear Lord before him, was moved to the depth of his being when he contemplated the masses of English people without Christ. Yet he ascribed to God alone his concern for the lost: 'And I thank God he gave unto me some measure of bowels and pity for their souls, which also did put me forward to labour with great diligence and earnestness, to find out such a word as might, if God would bless it, lay hold and awaken the conscience: in which also the good Lord had respect to the desire of his servant.' Bunyan's own testimony as an evangelist reveals his great awareness of God, for he dared not just speak the first word that came into his head, but sought out a word from God which would speak to, grip and awaken the conscience of the masses of the people. He clearly believed that some words of God were more relevant than others in speaking to the times in which he lived and to the heart of the people. Here Bunyan has much to teach us. He, who dressed Pilgrim in pictorial and allegorical clothing on his journey to the wicket gate, spoke very plainly when he preached the gospel, so that the ordinary people enjoyed listening to him. Again he tells us, 'I had not preached long before some began to be touched, and to be greatly afflicted in their minds at the apprehension of the greatness of their sin, and their need of Jesus Christ.' Like Spurgeon after him, he was amazed at his own early success. He just could not believe 'that God had owned in his work such a foolish one as I; and then came that word of God to my heart, with much sweet refreshment: "The blessing of them that are ready to perish is come upon me; yea I caused the widow's heart to sing for joy"' (Job 29:13).

Bunyan's words carry a humility and conviction rare in our day. He no doubt saw himself as Evangelist in *Pilgrim's Progress* with his back towards hell and his face towards heaven. He also saw himself as a man standing between God and a world 'ready to perish'. It is in this context that he wrote, 'I preached what I felt, what I smartingly did feel; even that under which my poor soul did groan and tremble to astonishment.' Such serious conviction characterized not only the manner in which he preached but the subject of his message. With singleness of purpose he reminds us, 'In my preaching of the word I took special notice of this one thing, namely, that the Lord did lead me to begin where his word begins — with sinners; that is, to condemn all flesh, and to open and allege that the curse of God by the law doth belong to and lay hold on all men as they come into the world, because of sin. Now this part of my work I fulfilled with great earnestness; for the terrors of the Law and guilt for my transgressions lay heavy on

my conscience.' Here he reminds us of Daniel Rowlands,
who for a period in his preaching of the law of God only
knew how to cut, but not to heal. For two years Bunyan
did not experience the healing balm of Gilead. Though his
voice daily cried out against sin and man's fearful state, the
evangelist needed to be evangelized himself. This the Lord
did in His mercy after those two long and eventful years.
'After which' he tells us, 'the Lord came in upon my soul
with some sure peace and comfort through Christ; for he
did give me many sweet discoveries of his blessed grace
through him.' Truly, like Wesley, his chains fell off, for he
had previously described himself as a chained evangelist.
He declares, 'I went myself in chains to preach to them in
chains; and carried that fire in my own conscience that I
persuaded them to be aware of.' Now his evangelistic preaching was altered. He still preached what he 'smartingly did
feel'; but it was no longer the fearful terror of the law but
a Christ known and experienced. For a full five years he
set Christ forth before all, in all the glories of His many
offices. Then one day, like Paul before him and many faithful men after him, he was cast into prison. Bunyan, very
much like Whitefield, must be called 'an awakener' for he
was for ever in his heart saying to the Lord, 'That if to be
hanged up presently before their eyes would be a means to
awaken them, and confirm them in the truth, I gladly
should be contented.' 'This one thing I do' is as fitting an
epitaph to John Bunyan as it was to the apostle Paul.
Avoiding disputes and strifes of any form among Christians,
with single conviction and aim, he writes, 'I saw my work
before me did run into another channel, even to carry an
awakening word: to that therefore did I stick and adhere.'
Bunyan was a pioneer evangelist in that he 'never endeav-
oured to, nor durst, make use of other men's lines'. Here
again he expresses the Pauline evangelistic principle: 'Yea,
so have I strived to preach the gospel, not where Christ was
named, lest I should build upon another man's foundation'
(Rom. 15:20).

Bunyan never embarked upon one of these evangelistic
journeys without what he called 'the going of God upon

my spirit, to desire that I might preach there'. Amazingly
he also 'observed that such and such souls in particular
have been strongly set upon my heart, and I stirred up to
wish for their salvation; and that those very souls have
after this been given as the fruits of my ministry'. How
remarkable was God's direction of Bunyan, not only to the
place to evangelize, but to the very people by name! That
it was not a figment of his imagination is borne out by the
salvation of those particular souls. Bunyan set out to invade
and conquer the worst places on earth for God. He boldly
asserts, 'My great desire in my fulfilling my ministry was to
get into the darkest places of the country, even among
those people that were farthest off of profession; yet not
because I could not endure the light, for I feared not to
show my gospel to any, but because I found my spirit did
lean most after awakening and converting work, and the
word that I carried did lean itself most that way also, "Yea,
so have I strived to preach the gospel, not where Christ was
named, lest I should build upon another man's foundation."' We may well ask, in the light of such evangelistic
zeal and his declared intent, did any man in his day more
perfectly fit the character of Evangelist than Bunyan the
'immortal dreamer' himself? Yet anyone who thinks that
preaching was an easy thing to him was never more wrong.
'In my preaching I have really been in pain' he unashamedly
admits, 'and have, as it were, travailed to bring forth
children to God; neither could I be satisfied unless some
fruits did appear in my work.' His suffering was aggravated
by the slanderous attacks made on him by his persecutors
who accused him of immorality and any other sin which
might defame his name and destroy his work. Yet God saw
to it that his work of evangelizing the country advanced so
well that the king himself came to hear of Bunyan. One
day King Charles II asked Dr Owen, the first Vice-Chancellor
of Oxford University, how a learned man, such as he, could
sit and listen to an illiterate tinker. He replied, 'May it
please your Majesty, could I possess that tinker's gift for
preaching I would most gladly relinquish all my learning.'
Even though John Bunyan was imprisoned for twelve years

in Bedford jail for preaching the gospel, his preaching did not completely cease. He so won his jailor's heart that he was sometimes allowed to preach, and so, putting down his pen from describing Pilgrim's progress he stepped forth, as it were, from the book's pages and again took on the role of Evangelist.

In London, where Bunyan had formerly preached with only a day's notice, the meeting-houses could not contain the congregation. It was nothing unusual to find twelve hundred people hanging on his every word, as he preached at seven in the morning on a working day in the cold of winter. Half of those who came had often to be turned away as he preached the gospel indoors in the meeting-house at the end of town. Tradition has it that in Reading he preached disguised as a carter, with whip in hand. He was certainly willing to be 'made all things to all men, that I might by all means save some'. Finally, on 2 December 1671, in the last year of his imprisonment Bunyan was called to be pastor of the little congregation at Bedford. Yet during that last year of imprisonment Bunyan proved to one and all that the Word of God is not bound. For it is recorded: 'He preached the gospel publicly at Bedford, and about the counties, and at London with great success, being mightily followed everywhere.' May the God of Bunyan give us such evangelists in the twentieth century, who will speak as dying men to dying men.

Although we may not agree with Carlile on everything, his words are relevant when he writes, 'Christian history is a good tonic for the depressed. Is it not true that whenever the evangelist for the day has uttered his voice, the hosts of waiting souls have rallied to the cross?' And again he says, 'Great evangelists have not been numerous. In England there have been at least four: Wycliffe, Wesley, Bunyan and Spurgeon. There may not be another. If so, there is the challenge of all who name the Name that was so dear to Spurgeon.' It is surely a truth that God has raised up at least one or two great evangelists and given them to the church in every succeeding century. What is equally wonderful is that God has similarly raised up one or two great men who have recognized the gifts of those evangelists.

## Eighteenth-century evangelists

Such a man was Bishop J. C. Ryle, who reviewed in retrospect the eighteenth-century evangelism of the church.
Having mentioned the magnificent efforts of England's
greatest evangelists, George Whitefield and John Wesley, he
links their names with those of other great evangelical
worthies of the day. He continues, 'To these two great
names we must add those of Grimshaw, Berridge, the first
Henry Venn, Rowlands, Romaine, Harvey, Toplady and
Fletcher of Madeley; every one of them, be it remembered,
a clergyman of the Church of England.' These were the
men who were chiefly used by God to bring about the
evangelical revival. How was their work done? Let Bishop
Ryle reply: 'The men who wrought deliverance for us . . .
were a few individuals, most of them clergymen, whose
hearts God touched about the same time in various parts
of the country. They were not wealthy or highly connected.
They were not put forward by any church, party, society
or institution. They were simply men whom God stirred
up and brought out to do his work, without previous concert, scheme or plan. They did his work in the old apostolic
way, by becoming the evangelists of their day. They taught
one set of truths. They taught them in the same way, with
fire, reality, earnestness, as men fully convinced of what
they taught. They taught them in the same spirit, always
loving, compassionate and, like Paul, even weeping, but
always bold, unflinching and not fearing the face of man.
And they taught them on the same plan, always acting on
the aggressive; not waiting for sinners to come to them,
but going after and seeking sinners; not sitting idle till
sinners offered to repent, but assaulting the high places of
ungodliness like men storming a breach, and giving sinners
no rest so long as they stuck to their sins.'
   Bishop Ryle also helpfully informs us of the methods of
the evangelists and the content of their preaching. He shows
that they preached everywhere: 'In the field, or by the
road-side, on the village-green, or in a market-place, in

lanes or in alleys, in cellars or in garrets, on a tub or on a table, on a bench or on a horse-block . . ., no place came amiss to them.'[3] Ryle concludes that they followed Augustine's maxim: 'A wooden key is not so beautiful as a golden one, but if it can open the door when the golden one cannot, it is far more useful.'

The eighteenth-century church in general did not discern God's gift of evangelists in the persons of Whitefield, Wesley and others, but rejected them and shut the doors of the church against them. John Wesley, like John Wycliffe before him, trained and encouraged itinerant preachers of the gospel. However, he did not exhort them to establish local independent evangelical churches of their converts, but rather grouped them in Methodist societies, and never in his lifetime encouraged separation from the Church of England, although for the most part it rejected his ministry and the preaching of his itinerants, as being contrary to the parochial system of the established church.

Perhaps some of the most significant words of Ryle here concerning these eighteenth-century evangelists are that 'they were not put forward by any church, party, society or institution'.

Great and amazing though the following century, the nineteenth, proved to be as regards missionary enterprise, the church retained its blindness to the gift of evangelist. In 1899, Eugene Stock, recounting the history of one of the greatest missionary societies after the first hundred years of missionary expansion, writes with incisive and devastating frankness: 'It is a humiliating thought that this one great commission which the church's risen Lord gave her to execute is the very thing she has not done. She has accomplished magnificent work. She has covered Christendom with splendid buildings for the worship of God. She has cared for the poor, the sick, the infirm, the aged, the young. She has taught the world to build hospitals and schools. But her Lord's one grand commission she has almost entirely neglected. It should have had the first place in her thoughts, sympathies and prayers. It has had the last place, if indeed it can be said to have had a place at all.

And all the while her Lord and Saviour "sitteth on the right hand of God the Father Almighty expecting" as the Epistle to the Hebrews expresses it. But a few of the church's members, sometimes as individuals, sometimes in bands and associations, have remembered their Lord's command and tried to do something. The story of one of these associations is the subject of the present volume.'

What an admission! What honesty! What frankness! Is this not the real truth that, because the church has largely forgotten and forsaken the great commission, it has fallen to 'individual bands and associations' to do it for her and in her place? Indeed, we must see these associations or missionary societies of the late eighteenth century as a condemnation of the church's failure to fulfil Christ's commission to evangelize the world.

How much better it would have been if, from the beginning, the church had retained the biblical name of evangelist rather than missionary, so that the primary purpose of evangelism might have been seen to be the preaching of the gospel, the saving of souls and the establishing of churches! It would then not have been so easily side-tracked into establishing schools and hospitals. These vital works could have been left to dedicated Christian teachers and doctors, while the church through its evangelists, or missionaries, concentrated on fulfilling its great commission.

## Nineteenth-century neglect

This terrible neglect by the church, of evangelism in general and the sending out of evangelists in particular, was the burden of Charles Haddon Spurgeon's heart. He dared to build his case on the very same passage that others have used to deliver the death-blow to the New Testament evangelist, namely Ephesians 4:11.

We shall conclude this brief historical sketch of evangelists through the centuries by quoting Spurgeon on this subject: 'Among men God's richest gifts are men of high vocation separated for the ministry of the gospel. From our ascended Lord come all true evangelists; these are they

who preach the gospel in divers places, and find it the
power of God unto salvation; they are founders of churches,
breakers of new soil, men of missionary spirit, who build
not on other men's foundations, but dig out for themselves.
We need many such deliverers of the good news where as
yet the message has not been heard. I scarcely know of any
greater blessing to the church than the sending forth of
earnest, indefatigable, anointed men of God, taught of the
Lord to be winners of souls.

'Who among us can estimate the value of George Whitefield to the age in which he lived? Who shall ever calculate
the price of a John Williams or a William Knibb? Whitefield
was made for the salvation of our country, which was going
down straight to pandemonium. Williams reclaimed the
Islands of the sea from cannibalism, and Knibb broke the
negro's chains. Such evangelists as these are beyond all price.

'Then come the pastors and teachers, doing one work in
different forms. They are sent to feed the flock; they abide
in one place and instruct converts which have been gathered
— these also are invaluable gifts of the Ascension of Jesus
Christ . . . whether you have pastors or evangelists they
exist for the good of the church of God. They ought to
labour for that end, and never for their own personal
advantage. Their power is the Lord's gift and it must be in
His way.

Brother, sister, if thou be in the body the least known
joint, rob not the body by indolence or selfishness, but use
the gift thou hast in order that the body of Christ may
come to its perfection. Yet since thou hast not great personal gifts, serve the church by praying. The Lord has
ascended to give us more evangelists, pastors and teachers.
He alone can give them; any that come without Him are
impostors. There are some prayers you must not pray, there
are others you may pray, but there are a few you must
pray. There is a petition which Christ has commanded us
to offer, and yet we very seldom hear it. It is this one,
'Pray ye therefore the Lord of the harvest, that He will
send forth labourers into His harvest.' We greatly lack evangelists and pastors. I do not mean we lack muffs, who

occupy the pulpit and empty the pews. I believe the market
has for many years been sufficiently supplied therewith;
but we lack men who can stir the heart, arouse the conscience and build up the church. The scatterers of flocks
may be found everywhere; the gatherers of them, how
many have we of such? Such a man at this day is more
precious than the gold of Ophir. The Queen can make a
bishop of the Established Church, but only the Lord can
send a bishop to the true church. Prelates, popes, cardinals,
vicars, prebends, canons, deans, the Lord has nothing to do
with. I see not even the name of them in His Word, but the
very poorest pastor whom the Lord ordains is a gift of His
ascending glory. At this moment we are deploring that in
the mission field our good men are grey. Duff, Moffat and
the like are passing from the stage of action. Where are
their successors? I was almost about to say, echo answers,
where? We want evangelists for India, for China, for all the
nations of the earth; and though we have godly fathers
among us, who are instructors in the faith, yet have we in
all our pastorates few men of eminence, who could be mentioned in the same day as the great Puritanic divines. If the
ministry should become weak and feeble among us, the
church richly deserves it, for this, the most important part
of her whole organization has been neglected more than
anything else. I thank God this church not only prayed for
ministers, but has proved the sincerity of her prayer by
helping such men as God has called, by affording them
leisure and assistance for understanding the way of God
more perfectly . . .

'Are we all to be builders on other men's foundations?
Have we none among us who can gather their own flocks?
In a three million city like this can any men say that
labourers for Christ are too many? Loiterers are too many,
doubtless, and when the church drives out the drones, who
shall pity them? While there remain hundreds of towns and
villages without a Baptist church and whole districts
of other lands without the gospel, it is idle to dream that
of evangelists and teachers we can have too many. No man
is so happy as he who presides over a flock of his own

gathering, and no pastor is more beloved than he who raised from ruin a destitute church and made it become a joy and praise in the earth. Pray the Lord to send true pastors and true evangelists. Christ procured them by His ascension. Let us not forget this. What! Shall it be thought that the blessings of the crucifixion are worth the having, and the blessings of the resurrection worth receiving, but the blessings of the ascension are to be regarded with indifference or even with suspicion? No; let us prize the gifts which God gives by His Son; and when He sends us evangelists and pastors let us treat them with loving respect. Honour Christ in every true minister; see not so much the man as his Master in him. Trace all gospel success to the ascended Saviour. Look to Christ for more successful workers. As they come receive them from His hands; when they come treat them kindly as His gifts, and daily pray that the Lord will send to Zion mighty champions of the faith.'[4]

Let us listen again to Charles Haddon Spurgeon's 'Country churches and Evangelization' speech at the Annual Meeting of the Home Missionary Society on 7 May 1878.

'I do not know whether your society is going to do it, but it lies upon my heart to recommend it — to send to the country churches evangelists to preach to them. Choose out two of the best men in your denomination, and send them into a district for a month, get their churches to give them up for a month, and let them stay in a district and work up a series of earnest-meetings, and the blessing it would be to humbler brethren who are labouring there no tongue can tell. I am sure that if some of the distinguished brethren whom you have in your midst would go into a country town and stay there, and work even for a week, it would give to your cause an impulse such as hardly anything else would give. I thank God for the work that was done by Messrs Moody and Sankey, and I am thankful for a good deal of irregular effort that has been put forth. But I devoutly wish that we had such effort in a regular manner, and that we had men officially recognized as evangelists who would go right through England from end to

end and stir up the people.' He goes on, 'We are always
forming new committees and altering our machinery.'
Later, he confesses, 'Dear me, we of the Baptist denomination and you of the Independent denomination have
been tinkering away for everlasting. We have always had
the man with a little bit of fire and a soldering pot for
mending up our old things; now let us boil something in
the pot — make some soup, do something. After all what
have our missionary societies done? A great thing, but
compared with what our Lord deserves, what a small thing
it is. God help us to get at it by some means, and that plan
of sending out leading men who have influence and power
to evangelize strikes me as likely to produce great results
in our country churches.'

## Local church evangelists

We make no excuse for quoting Spurgeon at length for he
alone puts the evangelist in his rightful scriptural and
church place. Yet, alas, apart from the efforts in his own
college to train evangelists, his words appear generally to
be unknown in the churches of the twentieth century. Yet
I believe that today we have, without exaggeration, the
greatest opportunity, possibly since apostolic times, of re-
establishing the gift of evangelist in our local evangelical
churches, for in the last half of this century we have been
led to see the importance of the doctrine of the local
church possibly as never before. We have rightly emphasized
the need for, and training of, pastors and teachers in those
churches. Do we not equally need to discern, train and
send out from our local churches God-given evangelists —
men who will preach the gospel in the unevangelized areas,
both urban and rural, where Christ is not named? If in
practice, one church at present finds difficulty in support-
ing an evangelist, is it not possible that a few like-minded
evangelical churches in a locality could band together under
God's guidance towards this great end? This would not
only lead in time to the total and regular evangelization of
our own land, but would also revolutionize in the truest

sense our modern conception of missions abroad. Without in any way belittling the efforts of the home missions of different denominations and fellowships, I am nevertheless convinced this work is ultimately the responsibility of each local evangelical church.

1. Eusebius: *Church History* (trans. by A.C. McGiffert), Book II chap.3, p.107
2. J. Bunyan: *Grace Abounding to the Chief of Sinners,* Evangelical Press edition, 1978, pp.106-112
3. J.C. Ryle: *Christian Leaders of the Eighteenth Century,* Banner of Truth Trust, p.22-23
4. C.H. Spurgeon: Metropolitan Tabernacle Pulpit vol.17, sermon no.982, 26 March 1871

# 3
# God-given pattern

## The church of God

The New Testament church realized that God had made
her the custodian of the gospel. We believe He put every
local church 'in trust' with His priceless jewel. Paul could
write to the church at Thessalonica, 'We were allowed of
God to be put in trust with the gospel' (1 Thess. 2:4).
They were not only amazed that God had allowed them to
be trusted with His gospel, but, surely, they were also aware
that one day God Himself was going to return to this world
and ask them, 'What have you done with My gospel?' That
is a terrifying question confronting the church of the
twentieth century, and indeed of every century. Before we
consider how we in our day are to discharge this 'trust', we
must ask how the New Testament church discharged that
same trust.

If we turn back to the first chapter of 1 Thessalonians
we are confronted by the pattern of local church evangelism.
We shall see the divine development in evangelism leading,
firstly, to the creation of the local church, and then to the
outreach of that newly-planted church into the unevangelized surrounding areas.

## The coming of God

The first great principle in the God-given pattern for evangelism is *the coming of God* to a community. Our eyes
focus on three men travelling towards a great Greek city,
equally famous for its monotheism and its paganism. Here

Jew and pagan rubbed shoulders as they made their way to their synagogue or temple, as isolated and unintegrated as city-dwellers have always been. Paul, Silas and Timothy had a single purpose, to win that city for God, and carried one sole possession, which they personally described as *'our* gospel'. They were coming to that city because God had first come to them individually in the gospel of Jesus Christ. They had not only believed the truth of it, but had embraced the Person, Jesus Christ. He, by the power of His death, had delivered them all from the power, pollution and penalty of sin. They were certain that the gospel 'worked' and that what it had done for them, it could do for all men everywhere. They carried nothing else with them because they needed nothing else to win this city for God. Yet they did not travel alone, for the God who had told them to 'go' to Thessalonica had equally promised them, 'Lo, I am with you.'

They began with those people who professed some knowledge of God. They therefore preached three sabbath days in the Jewish synagogue. Paul began 'as his manner was' by preaching. His method was to reason with the congregation 'out of the Scriptures' emphasizing the necessity for both the death of Christ and His resurrection from the dead. These three days of preaching were honoured by God and used as the means of salvation of some Jews, a much larger number of devout Greek men and, in particular, of some wealthy Greek women.

However, the God-given success of this evangelistic city mission was cut short by the envy and anger of those Jews who had rejected the preaching of the gospel. Suddenly, the sound of the gospel was replaced by that of uproar and revolt. The gathered congregation gave way to the assembling of the mob. These Jewish fanatics were unwilling to exchange the claims of their King Caesar for those of King Jesus. They were equally unwilling to have their comfortable world disturbed, let alone turned upside down, by these first-century evangelical preachers. Only one option was open to Paul and his companions: a night flight to Berea, there to preach another day. This historic account by Luke in the seventeenth chapter of the Acts of the Apostles is essential background reading for a true understanding of the opening chapter of 1 Thessalonians. It throws light on the coming of God to the city of Thessalonica in general, and in particular on the way God came through the ministry of Paul, Silas and Timothy and changed hell-bound heathens into heaven-bound Christians. We have seen clearly how they did this in the midst of a city in a state of uproar and revolt, set upon their destruction. Even in the teeth of revolution and rejection of their gospel, they held to their God-given pattern of evangelism, depending on the power of God's gospel. Now in retrospect they can attribute all the success to God. They remind these newly converted Thessalonians, 'Our gospel came not unto you in word only, but also in power, and in the Holy Ghost, and in much assurance' (1 Thess. 1:5).

Let us see that evangelism begins with *the preaching and the reception of the Word of God,* for the Thessalonians' own testimony was that they 'received the word of God which [they] heard . . . not as the word of men, but as it is in truth, the word of God, which effectually worketh also in you that believe' (1 Thess. 2:13). Effective evangelism begins when God Himself speaks through the preaching of His Word. It works effectively when the sinner no longer hears merely the voice of the preacher, but the voice of God. This is made possible only by the power of God accompanying the Word of God. Literally, God coming in power (1 Thess. 1:5) gained an entrance into the hardened hearts of these heathen Thessalonians. He came and placed the dynamic power of His Word alongside the seemingly impregnable heart of man. But is this really surprising from a God who says elsewhere, 'Is not my Word like a hammer which breaks the rocks in pieces?'

It is a paradox that, in an age when man is obsessed with the power game of atomic, hydrogen and neutron bomb warfare, he is almost totally ignorant of the greatest power in the world, the gospel of God. When placed beside the gospel these other things appear no more powerful than a damp Chinese squib! Even more to the point, while they are, tragically, weapons of world-destroying potency, God's gospel weapon is one of world-saving power. We may therefore be certain that the gospel that comes to men with power will create men of power.

This gospel also came *'in the Holy Ghost'*. No doubt it came in the power of the Holy Spirit which always characterized Paul's private and public utterances. For Paul's personal testimony of his own preaching was that 'my speech and my preaching was not with enticing words of man's wisdom, but in demonstration of the Spirit and of power' (1 Cor. 2:4). The Holy Spirit also made effective in the lives of the hearers God's eternal choice of them for salvation. For Paul later very wonderfully taught these Thessalonian converts to trace their salvation which took place in time, back to God in eternity. He showed them that 'God hath from the beginning chosen you to salvation through sanctification of the Spirit and belief of the truth: whereunto He called you by our gospel...' (2 Thess. 2:13,14).

Finally, the coming of God by the Word of God and the power of the Spirit of God created *Christians of certainty*. They were certain they were Christians. In a world of uncertainty, uncertain of its origin and destiny, Christians must be certain. If the Christian church is uncertain of its God and of His gospel, it will produce uncertain converts. That such a state of affairs already exists is sadly true, and we have only ourselves to blame since God has warned His church, 'If the trumpet give an uncertain sound who shall prepare for the battle?' Never was there a day when the need was greater than it is today to heed God's call to 'cry aloud, spare not, lift up thy voice like a trumpet and shew my people their transgression...' (Isa. 58:1).

## The following of God

We also learn from the first chapter of 1 Thessalonians that the sinner derives the assurance of his salvation from both the content of the gospel message and the character of the evangelists. This opens up the second great principle in the pattern of local church evangelism, namely *the following of God.* God comes to man, in order to be followed by man. Yet until man is assured of God he will never step out of line and follow God. The early church converts began to follow God because they not only trusted God, but they trusted the men who spoke to them from God. For Paul could write to them, 'Our gospel came not unto you in word only, but also in power, and in the Holy Ghost and in much assurance; as ye know what manner of men we were among you for your sake.'

It was the manner of the men of God which gave them assurance in God; so much so that Paul could testify, 'And ye became followers of us.' This is a truth that has largely been forgotten in our modern day of evangelism. The living of the evangelists is to be as holy and powerful as their preaching. Evidently, they lived in Thessalonica long enough to live lives worthy of imitation, for this word 'follower' literally means 'imitator'. We need to learn that if the life of the evangelist is not an imitation of the life of the Lord there will be no change in the life of the convert. Our lives must first be moulded by God. Only then will they be worthy of imitation. Elsewhere Paul exhorts the converts of Corinth, 'Be ye followers [imitators] of me even as I also am of Christ' (1 Cor. 11:1). Clearly the early church knew nothing of modern 'hit and run' or 'hit and miss' evangelism! In the early church the evangelists had to live long enough in a community to lead men to God by their lives as well as by their words. I wonder whether if unconverted sinners followed us to our place of work, to our haunts, to our pastimes, and lived in our homes, they would find Christ at the end of a week. If we, like Paul, called upon 'our' converts to imitate our life-style, what kind of person would we find facing us at the end of the day? Could we write to our converts as the writer of the Epistle to the Hebrews did, 'Remember them which have the rule over you [the leading ones] who have spoken unto you the word of God: whose faith *follow* considering the *end* of their conversation [way of life]. Jesus Christ the same yesterday, and today, and for ever' (Heb. 13: 7,8). The church today, alas, for the most part lacks evangelistic leaders of this kind. An evangelist is a God-given leader whose words come from God and whose life points to God. Our words, faith and way of life must all have the same *end*, Jesus Christ. He is a Jesus Christ who is the same. A life which derives its words, faith and life from abiding in Christ will be characterized by a sameness or consistency which Christ's life possessed on earth. If we possess the assurance of our personal salvation we shall declare that salvation with like assurance to a world uncertain of salvation.

## The living of God

We see developed here a divine progression in evangelism. The coming of God's men to a lost community is nothing less than the coming of God Himself in those men. As lost man begins to see God in those men, and is led to follow those men, he will find God for himself. Then God Himself will begin to live in that formerly lost community in a new way, in these newly-created and indwelt men of God. The coming of God leads to the following of God and then, thirdly, to the *living of God,* in the sense that we should become more like the God we follow. So Paul could write of the Thessalonian men of God, 'So that ye were ensamples [patterns] to all that believe in Macedonia and Achaia.' True evangelism leads to a change in the pattern of living in an individual life and in time in a whole community. God lived in the believers in Thessalonica in such a way that they became a pattern of godliness over a large area of pagan Greece. In Paul's own words these Thessalonian converts, like those at Corinth, were 'manifestly declared to be the epistle of Christ ministered by us, written not with ink, but with the Spirit of the living God' (2 Cor. 3:3). Though the life of God by His miraculous omnipresence is present everywhere, He is seen only in the saved lives of believers. Similarly, in a sense, He is heard only in the lives of saved men and women. For where God comes to a life and is followed, not only will He live and be seen in that life, but there will be a sounding out of God from that saved life.

As Paul let the lives of 'his' converts be seen for themselves, so he let their lips speak for themselves: 'For from
you sounded out the word of the Lord not only in
Macedonia and Achaia, but also in every place your faith
to God-ward is spread abroad; so that we need not to speak
any thing' (1 Thess. 1:8). In the last analysis the only lasting proof that God has entered into a particular place and
particular lives is the evidence of a turning to God from
the idols of our own creation.

## The witness to God

In considering the true pattern of evangelism it is essential
to see that in addition to the gift of evangelist in the local
church, all the members of the New Testament churches
evangelized. Indeed the Acts of the Apostles might equally
be titled the 'Acts of the early Christians'. For the early
church the personal witness of every member in the church
was the norm and not the exception. Furthermore, no place
was out of their reach and no situation too hard to handle.
The first glimpse we catch of Christians engaged in the
work of evangelism is inserted into the narrative between
the murdering of a preacher and the persecution of a local
church and the subsequent funeral service and the imprisonment of their fellow Christian men and women. We might
think this was hardly an opportune, let alone a wise,
moment to begin speaking for God! In fact, we are given to
understand that it was this series of events which triggered
off their personal evangelism, since Luke lays emphasis
upon the key word, *'therefore'*: 'Therefore they that were
scattered abroad went everywhere preaching the word'
(Acts 8:4). 'Preaching' is used here in the sense of telling
others of Christ in every town where the persecution drove
them. Later, Peter, who had so lamentably failed in his
greatest hour of opportunity of witness for Christ, showed
clearly that he had now learnt his lesson, for he encouraged
the scattered church to show forth the praises of God's salvation in the face of the persecution inspired by the
infamous Nero. He wonderfully uplifted those downtrodden

believers by showing them, not what they were in man's sight or in their own sight, but in God's sight. To God they were a choice people, royal people, holy people and a special people with a special mission in this present world (see 1 Peter 2:9,10). We may well ask, will the church of our own day ever see the greatness of its mission until it sees itself again in its own greatness in God's estimation? Only then will we see that our mission, like that of the church in Peter's day, is to 'show forth the praises (literally, the virtues) of him who hath called you out of darkness into His marvellous light'. Surely it is implied here that unless the individual Christian in the church realizes from what he has been saved he will never see the fearful plight of the people he is seeking to save.

One day, as I stood at the face of a coal mine in Wales and looked down the dark shaft, I saw as never before in my life, the picture of God calling down into the darkness and bringing people up into the marvellous light of His day of grace. The church of God was once in the darkest place, blackened by the grime of wickedness and ignorance, and in alienation and enmity towards God. We were darker then Welsh coal! If we have never seen that then we have never seen from what we have been saved, or, even worse, we have never been saved at all. In fact, the apostle Paul reminded the Ephesian believers, 'Ye were darkness.' The divine logic and reasoning of both the inspired apostles Paul and Peter is that no one will ever appreciate the marvellous light of God's salvation until he has seen the fearful darkness of his personal sin. The lighthouse of Christ's salvation is nothing to unfallen angels living in the light of God's perfect presence, but it is everything to us mariners in the tempestuous sea of sin. The personal knowledge of salvation from darkness and entrance into God's marvellous light are God's essential qualifications for the work of personal evangelism. For only such a person is a proof that God still saves sinners today in the twentieth century. Our chief credential is that by faith we have climbed the hill of Calvary and proved that there is still 'power, power, wonder-working power in the blood of Calvary'. Only a man who has been up there can come down and show forth the praises and saving virtues of such a God and Saviour to our sinsick and benighted world.

## Ready for God

We cannot begin to call a world back to God if we have not been moved ourselves to respond to God's call to faith and repentance towards Him. That is evangelism; that is where it begins and ends. Only then are we ready to speak for God. Indeed, it is both salutary and interesting to notice how much time the apostle Peter spends in his first letter dealing with the life of those who are to evangelize, rather than those who are to be evangelized. I wonder sometimes whether we have turned the order the wrong way round.

God gave Peter discernment to see that the chief factor holding back these early Christians from witnessing for God was the fear of man. As we have already seen, when Peter wrote, the world at large lived in fear of the infamous Roman Emperor Nero, who was particularly set on the extermination of Christians. Yet while Nero was carrying out his hellish plan, Peter assures them that the man of God, called to evangelize the world, may be characterized by both fearlessness and happiness. The reason for this he is not slow to put forward! 'But if ye suffer for righteousness' sake happy are ye' (1 Peter 3:14). The Christian who witnesses to God's righteousness must be willing sometimes to suffer terribly for that righteousness at the hands of an unrighteous world. Quickly, as if he read their minds and anticipated their reply, Peter adds, 'And be not afraid of their terror, neither be troubled.'

There is no doubt that the fear of man has often crippled the church's witness and silenced its tongue for God. Peter is indeed recalling to mind the fear which characterized the church of God in Isaiah's day, centuries before Christ's incarnation. God's people were in grave danger of being contaminated by the fear of the unbelieving world surrounding them, which had driven the king of that day and his people to seek an ungodly alliance and confederacy with the evil nations around them, believing that there was safety in numbers. But God directed Isaiah and, through him, God's people to a better fear. He instructed them, 'Neither fear ye their fear, nor be afraid. Sanctify the Lord of Hosts himself; and let him be your fear, and let him be your dread' (Isa. 8:12,13). This command is relevant, however one interprets 'their fear', that is the world's fear. In Isaiah's day, or in Peter's, as well as in our day, it may refer objectively to the fear of what man will do to us. It strikes right at the root of society. At the worst the world wonders whether there will be a third world war. Will man exterminate himself by the neutron bomb or some more deadly device to come? On a more personal level, it may be the fear of being homeless and forsaken by those we love. It may take the form of the fear of the future, the fear of the unknown, the fear of failure and, most of all, the fear of death. Before we dare to address the world we must realize its fearful state. Yet 'their fear' is not merely an objective fear; the fear from without brings fear within our hearts. It creates a spirit of disquiet and dejection. Both prophet and apostle encourage us not to fear in the way that the man of the world fears. Far from this being a digression from the matter of personal evangelism, it emphasizes the preparation of the witness. We must not objectively fear what the world fears, nor must we subjectively fear in the way the world fears. Yet that is easier said than done.

## The fear of God

It is at this point that the apostle Peter introduces in a sense a third fear, the fear of God. He instructed these Christians negatively, 'Be not afraid of their terror, neither be troubled', but positively, 'Sanctify the Lord God in your hearts.' We cannot truly begin to evangelize a fearful world until our own human fear has been conquered by a divine fear — the fear of God has replaced the fear of man. Truly, 'the fear of the Lord is the beginning of knowledge,' and particularly of the knowledge of how to evangelize. As the hymn-writer correctly says, 'Fear Him, ye saints, and you will

then have nothing else to fear.' We may ask, 'How are we
to reach and maintain such an attitude as we seek to live,
let alone to evangelize, in the midst of such a world?' The
answer is constantly to learn and relearn David's maxim,
'What time I am afraid, I will trust in the Lord' (Ps. 56:3).
It means we have to centre our hearts upon God Himself.
As Isaiah wrote, 'Sanctify the Lord of Hosts himself; and
let him be your fear, and let him be your dread.' A holy
fear of God Himself will drive out the unholy fear of man
from our hearts, whether man appears in the form of
nations set on our destruction or in those who cruelly
threaten and maltreat us on a personal level. In down-to-
earth practical terms, the fear of God and the fear of man
cannot live together in the same heart or life. Again, the
fear of God is an uplifting, joyous fear, a fear which
respects and does not reject the person it fears. It is a fear
which is full of reverence, not revulsion, for its object. This
is the first God-given requirement for the Christian who
would evangelize His world. Only then are we ready to
speak for God. Surely there was never meant to be such a
person as a silent, or a secret Christian.

Having instructed the believers concerning the preparation of the witness, Peter now emphasizes his readiness, for
he is to 'be ready always' to speak for God. When I was
first a Christian, I truly tried to make, and sometimes, I am
afraid, to force opportunities to speak for God — often
with disastrous results. There came a day when that gem of
a book *Adolphe Monod's Farewell* came into my hand.
Adolphe Monod in his day was the greatest and most
famous preacher in France, and then suddenly he was cut
down by illness and forced to exchange his pulpit for a bed.
But there, often to only a handful of people, he poured
out his heart. It was the burning passion of a man who not
only wanted his brethren to know his dying regrets, but
was concerned that they might not make the same mistakes.
One of these mistakes seems to have concerned his use of
time for God. He had discovered that we are 'his workman-
ship, created in Christ Jesus unto good works, which God
hath before ordained that we should walk in them' (Eph.

2:10). Monod's vital contribution, or rather Paul's before him, was that we are not required to make, let alone force, the opportunities to speak for God, but that they are daily prepared for us by God. This takes all the tension and stress out of personal evangelism. It does not, on the other hand, make us slothful, but prayerfully waiting to be guided by God to the person He has prepared for us, to whom we are to have the honour of speaking for God. The sheer honesty of Monod has in measure revolutionized my view of personal evangelism. God has prepared the person, the place and time where we are to speak for Him. We need daily to place our whole lives in His hands and ask Him to guide us to prepared hearts. We should tell God daily of our willingness to speak for Him.

I have felt constrained to tell the following story so that the readers of this book may equally be challenged. Some time ago, I was speaking for a day to university students, prior to embarking on a mission in the city where I minister. I finished by recounting what I have mentioned here. When I returned home my wife informed me of a message concerning an eighty-six-year old atheist lady who was dying and apparently afraid to die. Within half an hour that genuine atheist was converted and singing in a shrill voice, 'I know that my Redeemer liveth,' a hymn she had not sung since she was a teenager. For the next ten days all who had known her as a very hardened atheist were bound to acknowledge the amazing grace of God. I have no doubt in my heart that God vindicated the truth I sought to teach those students, that God has someone for them to speak to each day. He proved it to me within an hour of uttering those words! My friend, there are people living in the place where you live, waiting to hear a word of God through your lips.

Perhaps you say, 'But what am I to speak of?' The apostle leaves us in no doubt as to the content of our confession. We are to 'be ready to give an answer'. The Greek word here is 'apology'. This does not carry with it the modern meaning of making an excuse for something, but rather of giving a defence of the gospel, or a defence of our faith, of our hope in Christ, before a world which generally considers it false. The great apostle Paul could say, 'I am set for the defence of the gospel' and truly he was not ashamed to make that defence before a king, a young woman in the grip of the occult, or the intellectuals of Greece.

This leads us naturally to consider to whom we are to speak about Christ. Peter gives us the answer when he says, 'To every man that asketh you'. We must be ready to speak to all men for the simple reason that 'all have sinned and come short of the glory of God'. Often our missions have been solely directed towards the poor and the ignorant of the world, as if they were in greater need of God than the educated and the rich. Yet sin can be hidden behind mink as easily as rags, and found in the mansions of this world as well as in more humble dwellings. No wonder Paul had a world mission of evangelism, nor did his true understanding of the doctrine of election silence his lips from declaring, 'God . . . now commandeth all men every where to repent' (Acts 17:30). For him the understanding of the universality of sin led him to make a universal call for repentance, and to be ready always to give an apology. Let this teach us to be ready to speak to all men everywhere. Talk to your neighbour, that person you daily sit beside in the train, that couple with whom you have coffee in your home, or that lonely person who needs to hear you speak of your hope in God. Some will thank God for your doing so as long as they live. It is true to say that some of you reading this book have opportunities to testify of God's salvation to people who would never think of entering a church building, or who through force of circumstances may not be able to do so. Many years ago, I sat up to nearly two o'clock in the morning trying to finish a crossword. The clue was 'single knocker'. At last it dawned: opportunity. Yes, even in evangelism opportunity sometimes only 'knocks' once as far as speaking to immortal souls is concerned. Truly the apostle exhorted the believers of his day to be 'redeeming the time because the days are evil' which, in a nutshell, means 'buying up the opportunity' for God.

For it is only when a man sees Christ in your life that he will realize what is lacking in his own.

## The hope of God

Now the apostle continues, 'Be ready to give a defence to every man that asketh you a reason of the hope that is in you.' This can be better rendered, 'to every man that asketh you an account' or 'a statement of the hope that is in you'. We are not to witness simply because we want to, or feel we ought to, but because of the hopeless state of the world. The church of God has been entrusted by God with the only message of true hope for a hopeless world. Every true Christian can declare that there was a time when he had no hope, simply because he did not know Christ as his Saviour. For God reminds us that we were as unbelievers 'at that time . . . without Christ' and goes on to say, 'having no hope, and without God in this world' (Eph. 2:12). Surely this lays upon us as a church in the twentieth century the tremendous urgency not only of reminding the world of its hopelessness, but even more of showing that the reason for its hopelessness is its Christlessness. Equally, we must make plain to the unbeliever that the rejection of Christ as a personal Saviour from our sinfulness renders us not only hopeless in this world, but also in the world to come. Yet hope is found not merely as the fruit of the crucifixion of Christ, but also of the resurrection.

To Paul the resurrection was not so much a doctrine to be delineated or debated (as it has been too much in modern society by the church) but a message of hope to be declared to the hopeless. For that supreme reason he preached before great and small the hope of the resurrection (Acts 23:6). But also to the true believer in Christ he wondrously and comfortingly showed that the indwelling Christ was a sure foretaste of glory. No wonder A.W. Tozer preached what was to be his last great sermon on these immortal words of hope: 'Christ in you, the hope of glory' (Col. 1:27). Paul's love for perishing humanity was such that he dared not let man die with an incomplete understanding, or a false hope in Christ. If that hope did not extend on into eternity, if it was extinguished at death, it was vain and useless, so he wrote powerfully, 'If in this life only we have hope in Christ, we are of all men most miserable' (1 Cor. 15:19).

If the church does not show the world the hopelessness and miserableness of man apart from Christ, and does not freely offer God's glorious way of salvation, it not only fails man, but, what is far more dreadful, it fails the 'God of hope'. No wonder Peter commenced his first letter by praising and thanking God for this living hope He had brought to a dying and perishing world. This world, and sometimes even the church, has forgotten a God who 'according to his abundant mercy hath begotten us again unto a lively hope by the resurrection of Jesus Christ from the dead, to an inheritance incorruptible, and undefiled, and that fadeth not away, reserved in heaven for you . . .' (1 Peter 1:3,4).

## The man of God

Finally the apostle deals with the manner in which we are to speak to people about God. He reminds us of the twin qualities of 'meekness and fear'. To the man of the world who arrogantly boasts, 'We have to be cruel to be kind,' meekness must appear more of a vice than a virtue. Yet there is a divine compelling magnetism in genuine meekness which is irresistible in drawing sinners to God. We are not therefore surprised that the man of God who led the flock of God through a wilderness for forty years was 'very meek'. Yet Moses was but a pale shadow of Christ to whom he pointed across the centuries. Yes, men will always follow a meek man of God. For the meekest Man of all called a sin-worn, weary and burdened world to Him, and that call to sinful man was motivated by meekness. Evangelism is the meek call of God to proud and burdened man. He still calls, 'Come unto Me, all ye that labour and are heavy laden, and I will give you rest' or better, 'I will rest you' (Matt. 11:28). We come and exchange our weary labour and our burden of sins for soul rest at the cross. We exchange our burden of sin for His yoke, for the burden of serving such a God — a burden which is easy to accomplish and light to lift for God.

But this can happen only when we come to Christ and know what He means when He says, 'Learn of Me.' It is nothing less than to be introduced to the very heart of God. Evangelism is not only the call of the meek and lowly heart of God, but it involves coming and learning the meekness and lowliness of the heart of God. Before we can be meek evangelists we must first have partaken of the heart of the Meek Evangelist. Meekness is a prerequisite in the heart of the evangelist because the One we represent is meek. No wonder then that the only man who can lift the fallen is a spiritual man. That man is meekness itself. Such men God needs. Such men God must have. Only when we have come to the heart of Christ's meekness and been conquered and compelled by it, will we hear Him say, 'Ye which are spiritual, restore such an one in the spirit of meekness' (Gal. 6:1). We have nothing to give to the world from Christ more than we have received ourselves. We therefore also have nothing to boast of, for we are no better than the people to whom we go. Only Christ has made us different. Let us go, then, with humility and love, desiring only to tell them of the hope which God in His mercy has given us.

Finally, God requires that we go 'with fear', fearing not the person to whom we speak, but rather the God of whom, for whom and with whom we speak. That is sufficient to make any man tremble with holy wonder every time he climbs the pulpit steps, or knocks on the door of a lost world. As that door opens we speak with God standing by our side, not only hearing every word, but mercifully putting His words in our mouths to speak for Him. Well may we speak with godly fear when we realize that we are God's messengers of hope, speaking of the hope of salvation He alone can bestow, and with a due realization that God is at our shoulder. It is one thing to know, 'There was a man sent from God whose name was John', but it is quite another thing to know, 'There is a man sent from God whose name is . . .' Let each of us go and be that man!

# 4
# God-given proclamation

Evangelism is concerned not only with what man is to hear about God, but *how* he is to hear it. The Bible has as much to say about the manner of the presentation of the gospel as the matter of it. Evangelism in a sense begins with a question mark: 'How then shall they call on him in whom they have not believed?' This is immediately followed by a further question which brings us right to the heart of the gospel proclamation: 'And how shall they believe in him of whom they have not heard?' (Rom. 10:14.) Here is the very sequence of the salvation of a soul. It begins with a man somewhere calling on God for salvation, because he has believed the gospel that he has heard with his own ears. But there is one more basic question we have omitted: '*How* shall they hear?' Some today would say, as others have said before them, that it does not really matter how, just so long as they hear. Their point is that it is the gospel that matters, and not the manner in which it is presented to man. If this was merely a human question, then I suppose, in a sense, it might have a human answer, but it is God's question which God must answer for man. God's question, 'How shall they hear?' concludes with the words: 'without a preacher'. A preacher is clearly God's man. He is literally a herald of God to bring man to hear the gospel in order that he may believe it and call upon God for salvation (Rom. 10:11-14). Yet God asks one final question through the apostle Paul: 'And how shall they preach, except they be sent?' Is there a more wonderful description of such a man than the one which God gave of John the Baptist: 'There was a man sent from God whose name was

John'? Here then is the commencement of proclamation. This picture is one which we may draw of God at the opening of every new day of evangelistic opportunity. For He informs us, 'Since the day that your fathers came forth out of the land of Egypt unto this day I have sent unto you all my servants the prophets, daily rising up early and sending them' (Jer. 7:25).

## Custodians of the gospel

It is time now to consider these God-given and God-sent preachers of the gospel in action. The date is around A.D.51. The place is Thessalonica. The prevailing atmosphere is one of idolatry. How are such pagans in this sophisticated Greek world to be brought to hear the gospel? We might think such a situation demands a special method. We have deliberately selected this particular evangelistic enterprise for closer consideration because the presentation of the gospel is described in such detail. The evangelists preached out of a sense of being custodians of the gospel. They clearly spoke to the Thessalonians as men who had been given a special trust by God. In their record of their mission they wrote, 'But as we were allowed of God to be put in trust with the gospel, even so we speak' (1 Thess. 2:4). They realized that they were neither the creators nor the inventors of the gospel, but custodians of it. This awareness clearly governed both what they said and the way they said it. Such an overriding trust will not permit of any interference with it, nor any alteration to it. It is an awe-inspiring thought that God has committed His gospel to our custody. Paul, Silas and Timothy describe the glorious entrance of the gospel with divine authority. This gospel venture was characterized by boldness. They could declare, 'We were bold in our God to speak unto you the gospel of God' (1 Thess. 2:2). They spoke not merely *of* God, but *in* God. They preached from the basis of their union with God. We are left in no doubt as to the evidence of the authority which accompanied and honoured their bold preaching: they could describe its impact upon the Thessalonians themselves. They recorded, 'They themselves shew of us what manner of entering in we had unto you, and how ye turned to God from idols to serve the living and true God' (1 Thess. 1:9). There can hardly be any greater proof of the power of God to change men's lives through God-given preaching.

### Character of the gospel

Next, they inform us of the way in which they accomplished this. They describe explicitly the glorious character of their gospel presentation. They could so easily have been tempted to adopt the 'in' methods of communication used by the fakers and philosophers in the world of their day, for these people, too, had their converts. But for the early gospel preachers a greater and higher principle was at stake, namely, the character of God. 'For our exhortation was not of deceit, nor of uncleanness, nor in guile' (1 Thess. 2:3). The very nature of God brought a negative emphasis into their evangelistic exhortation. It was 'not of deceit'. It was not out of character with God. It did not seduce. It did not use deception. It did not delude men about God. The word used here by the apostles describes a wandering planet, giving the sense that their presentation did not lead people to wander from the path of truth.

Secondly, their method of communication was not marked by uncleanness. It was 'not of uncleanness' because they represented and were to reflect a God who is 'of purer eyes than to behold evil, and canst not look on iniquity' (Hab. 1:13). There was no room for impurity of motive in their evangelism nor for lewdness in presentation. There was no place for using any media or methods which would excite, or play on the emotions of their hearers.

A third negative constraint was laid upon these evangelists in order to distinguish their method of communication from the deceitful and immoral methods used by the communicators of their day. They refused to use the most persuasive human methods, in case they misrepresented God and deceived man: their method was not 'in guile'. This meant that, when they preached, they did not set out with the aim of capturing an audience. They reckoned this to be both trickery and fraud. They dared not entrap people, dishonour God nor falsify His gospel. The early church clearly realized the danger of a gospel proclamation which could trick people and bait them into belief. There could be no place for the adulteration of the gospel. This attitude has been summarized in Paul's words: 'But [having] renounced the hidden things of *dishonesty* . . . nor handling the word of God *deceitfully;* but by manifestation of the truth commending ourselves to every man's conscience in the sight of God' (2 Cor. 4:2). These Thessalonian converts were won to Christ as much by the truthfulness of the character of the proclaimers as by the truth of the proclamation. This is made even plainer in that the declared intent of the apostles was so to 'speak not as pleasing men, but God, which trieth our hearts' (1 Thess. 2:4). This calls to mind Oliver Cromwell's prescription that 'the people should have what's for their good, not what pleases them'. The early preachers of the gospel were primarily concerned to please God and not men. Their method of communicating the gospel was not therefore aimed at entertaining sinners, but converting them. It did not seek by any means to create joy or happiness without prior conviction of sin. Holiness, not happiness was the hallmark of their evangelistic method. They clearly saw happiness or joy as, at best, a by-product of the gospel and not its primary purpose.

To those who would argue, 'But what of the joy promised to the world at the coming of Christ?' we would answer that they have missed the main thrust of the angel's message. It was not only: 'I bring you good tidings of great joy, which shall be to all people', but the cost and condition of that joy is knowing that 'unto you is born . . . a Saviour, which is Christ the Lord' (Luke 2:10,11). Yes, the joy of the world can be known without a Saviour, but the joy of God can only be known after salvation by God from our sins. Even in heaven the joy that the angels experience is over man's salvation from sin. For we read, 'I say unto you, that likewise joy shall be in heaven over one sinner that repenteth, more than over ninety and nine just persons, which need no repentance' (Luke 15:7). The only happiness the early preachers, like their Lord, desired to promote was the happiness of the pure in heart (Matt. 5:8).

These proclaimers of the gospel, as they went to present the gospel to the people of their day, never lost sight of a cloud always hovering over man — the cloud of God's wrath. For with their spiritual eyes they saw that 'the wrath of God abideth on him' (John 3:36). They saw that wrath was ever present every time they preached. The unbeliever was like a prisoner already in a condemned cell. In God's estimation the world is a great prison because 'he that believeth not is condemned already' (John 3:18). Yet their message was that God loved the world when it was perishing under the present cloud of God's wrath and already condemned (John 3:16).

Those who proclaimed this gospel at Thessalonica therefore believed that the purpose of gospel proclamation was to deliver people 'from the wrath to come' (1 Thess. 1:10). This means that any presentation of the gospel which sets out to please men is totally ignorant of the true character of God in His holiness and the true character of man in his sin. Clearly it is cruel to seek to please men who are dead in sin (Eph. 2:1) just as no doctor in his right mind would think of giving sweets instead of medicine to someone who was dangerously ill. An evangelist is a man who, by sheer definition, has seen the sinfulness and the total depravity of the sinner to be too profound and deep-seated a condition to be treated superficially.

### Aim of the gospel

Paradoxically, as it may seem, the aim of the gospel is to please not our human hearers but our heavenly God. True evangelism has the same aim as the One it seeks to portray. The secret of Christ's life must become the secret of the preacher's life. Christ summed up His declared aim in these amazing words: 'And he that sent me is with me: . . . for I do always those things that please him.' And we are left in no doubt that a ministry which is pleasing to God will always be honoured to the salvation of our hearers, for immediately it is recorded: 'As He spake these words, many believed on Him' (John 8: 29,30).

The preacher of the gospel aims, then, at pleasing God by preaching with a view to creating repentance and faith in Christ as Saviour. 'But without faith it is impossible to please Him' (Heb. 11:6). He never allows himself to forget that 'faith cometh by hearing, and hearing by the word of God' (Rom. 10:17). Is it not time for us as proclaimers and presenters of the gospel to examine whether we have not sought mainly to please the hearts of our hearers and have nearly totally forgotten the God who tries our hearts?

For this very reason when Paul, Silas and Timothy daily faced the permissive idol-worshipping pagans of their day, they never sought to flatter them. They dared not seek the adulation of man. Remarkable though it may seem they never once fell to the sin of flattery. For they declare, 'Neither at any time used we flattering words' (1 Thess. 2:5). The very mention of flattery by the greatest preacher in the then known world is surely an implicit confession of the great temptation to use flattery which every proclaimer of the gospel faces. It is a temptation that will be constantly with the preacher as long as he preaches and wherever he preaches, to the day he dies. One of the subtlest ways of flattering man is to communicate the gospel in the way he wants, rather than the way he needs. It is to seek to play up to him, to win him by words, to impress him by our wisdom. The motive may be sincere, but the result will be to render the gospel of God ineffective. Wherever Paul preached we believe he was tempted to flatter, since, confronted by the task of evangelizing the Corinthians, he describes his manner of gospel proclamation in these words: 'For Christ sent me not to baptize, but to preach the gospel: not with wisdom of words, less the cross of Christ should be made of *none effect*' (1 Cor. 1:17). Flattery removes the offence of Christianity, namely the cross, or else it replaces the wood of the cross with gold. It may remove the offensive blood of the cross and replace it with attractive jewels. It may encourage us to place the cross on our 'altars' or wear it round our necks, but never to preach it from our pulpits or take it up daily in a life of self-denial. The danger is just as great today as it was in Paul's day of producing a crossless Christianity whose flattering appeal creates fans, but not followers.

Paul did not fall to the temptation to flatter man, either at Thessalonica or at Corinth, because he determined to *bear* 'the testimony of *God*' to man. He tells us how he might have evangelized Corinth, but did not. 'I . . . came not with excellency of speech or of wisdom, declaring unto you the testimony of God' (1 Cor. 2:1). No doubt if he had come to testify of Paul, and not of God, his ways would have been those of the proud, bigoted Saul of Tarsus, graduate of Jerusalem University and a convert from the aristocracy. These things Paul had put behind him for ever. He considered them nothing more than dung and worthless refuse when placed beside the excellency of the knowledge of Christ (Phil. 3:4-14). Similarly, as a preacher he did not preach the attainments of Paul but those of Christ. The declared resolution of his preaching was, 'For I determined not to know anything among you, save Jesus Christ, and him crucified' (1 Cor. 2:2). His preaching did not portray his own personality, nor his ability or self-confidence, but on the contrary he confesses, 'And I was with you in weakness, and in fear, and in much trembling' (1 Cor. 2:3).

I shall never forget visiting the church in Kidderminster where saintly Richard Baxter preached in the seventeenth century. I learnt that day the secret of the man who declared, 'I preached as a dying man to dying men.' I came to the pillar on which one could see where his pulpit once had been. I suddenly discerned the faint words remaining on the pillar: 'We preach not ourselves, but Christ Jesus the Lord' (2 Cor. 4:5). He had learnt Paul's secret: 'And my speech and my preaching was not with enticing words of man's wisdom, but in demonstration of the Spirit and of power' (1 Cor. 2:4).

Does not this teach us that the man who would proclaim God to man must first have learnt his own weakness in the presence of the Almighty God and have trembled in the fear of such a God? Such a man would never dare to entice men with man's wisdom. Such a preacher and proclaimer God is bound to honour with the demonstration of His power. Perhaps we, in the twentieth century, need to ask ourselves, not so much, 'What is wrong with our preaching?' but 'What is wrong with us preachers?' Are we too strong for God to use? Are we too wise for God to use?

Paul leaves us in no doubt why he preached as he did: because he knew the fearful end of preaching was as much revealed in a negative purpose as in a positive one. Men would either worship the words of the preacher and rest their faith in his wisdom, or would trust in the power of the Almighty. Preaching always achieves an end, either human or divine. The gospel purpose of preaching is that 'your faith should not stand in the wisdom of men, but in the power of God' (1 Cor. 2:5).

These early preachers to the Thessalonians, like those to the Corinthians, never used flattery, nor did they throw a cloak of covetousness (1 Thess. 2:5) over the true nature of God or the fearful need of man in this world. True preaching is a declaration of the God who has revealed Himself to man, in order that the hidden condition of man may be revealed. The idea behind a preacher's using a 'cloak of covetousness' is using a pretext either to hide the true state of affairs or to give a false impression of the true God. False preaching is characterized by covetousness or greed. Spiritual greed desires to gain a reputation, or a congregation, literally to capture an audience. It will often hide the justice of God in order not to lose the people. It will throw a cloak over holiness and hell. It will put in the 'shop window' of the church nothing but so-called 'love' and an appealing picture of Christ and the Christian life. Yet when someone 'enters the shop' he will discover that he has been deceived. The God of the Saturday night gospel service has lost His smile by the time of the Sunday morning 'worship service'. But then we are told that the end justifies the means. We use all means to win some!

## Witnesses of the gospel

Why did these early proclaimers of the gospel not fall to
the level of the communicators of their day? Their answer
is short but solemn: 'God is witness' (1 Thess. 2:5). As
they prepared their messages they were aware of God looking over their shoulders, so to speak. As they stood up to
proclaim Christ, they knew God was in the congregation.
That is why Paul adds, 'Nor of men sought we glory.' A
God-given proclaimer never seeks fans for himself, but
followers for his God. I remember a Christian periodical
once describing a preacher as 'up and coming'. He did
'arrive' but he has long since been 'down and gone'. Popu-
larity and pride have slain far more preachers than damn-
able heresy any day of the week! And Paul adds that such
preachers are burdensome or heavy: 'We might have become
burdensome', he admits. However, they avoided that pitfall
by coming to their congregations as nurses do to a ward
full of children, motivated by true affection (1 Thess.
2:7,8). Again, rather than drawing attention to themselves
in self-glorification, they gave themselves to the people in
self-denial because they were dear to them. That depth of
care and concern for the souls of their hearers was
supremely expressed in preaching the gospel to men. They
reasoned with their congregation: 'Because we would not
be chargeable unto any of you, we preached unto you the
gospel of God' (1 Thess. 2:9).

How different is the reasoning of many in our day!
Because they do not want to upset or offend the people,
or to put them off, they are afraid to preach to them.
They sing of Christ, they recite Christ, they dramatize
Christ, they dance Christ, but less and less do they preach
Christ. Yet Paul argues, 'The dearer you are to me, the
more I will preach to your souls'.

So precious were the souls of the lost unconverted
Thessalonians, and so hard was the work of evangelism,
that he equated preaching with labour and the pains of a
woman giving birth (1 Thess. 2:9). He knew nothing of the
world of entertainment evangelism and the pop concert.

He knew nothing of part-time evangelism; for him preaching was 'labouring night and day'. Someone has got it wrong! Are we men of God enough to ask, 'Have I?'

## The God of the gospel

Paul could also remind his converts how differently the evangelists lived from the world around them. They could call up their new converts as witnesses to the fact that they had lived out God before them. They reminded them, 'Ye are witnesses, and God also, how holily and justly and unblameably we behaved ourselves among you that believe' (1 Thess. 2:10). We have seen earlier that they could testify to their converts prior to their conversion: 'Ye know what manner of men we were among you for your sake. And ye became followers of us, and of the Lord' (1 Thess. 1:5,6).

Too often in modern evangelism we have forgotten the principle and the power of the changed life, the difference which God produces in a converted man, in his beliefs, tastes, pastimes and pursuits. If the man of the world sees that we are no different from him, why should he become a Christian? It is time we faced God's Word in this vital aspect of evangelism.

We must represent God as He is. The God of the early church was unchanging, so the message of the early church came over loud and consistently clear: 'This then is the message which we have heard of Him . . . God is light, and in Him is no darkness at all' (1 John 1:5). The New Testament church assumed the existence of God and declared the character of God.

Have we not often allowed the character of man or our own characters to determine the way the gospel is presented in our day? We assume that, after all, God is very like ourselves. He has either become an extension of us, or more often an extension of the in figure of the day. About a century ago the popular view of God was rather like a grander picture of the venerable Victorian grandfather, with long white hair and impeccable manners. No doubt he sat on a cloud with a harp in his hand. Yet are we any better? For many he is distinctly younger, but still has long hair of a different colour, and has merely changed his instrument. He is the 'God' who is a best seller and worth queueing up to watch every night, but not to worship. This so-called 'God' changes with every new cult or in figure. He is certainly not the God of heaven. He is certainly not Jesus Christ 'the same yesterday, today and for ever'. Some years ago, I found myself preaching in a service with the predominant heavy-beat gospel backing. As I drove home I turned to a young person in my car and asked, 'What would you have done if the Lord Jesus Christ had walked in?' The answer came back without a moment's hesitation: 'I would have got under my seat.'

Does our evangelism entertain and embarrass or glorify God and save souls? The glory of God and the salvation of men are both biblical ingredients of true living evangelism. A writer gave some sound advice on this matter a long time ago: 'Remember them which have the rule over you, who have spoken unto you the word of God: whose faith follow, considering the end of their conversation [way of life]. Jesus Christ the same yesterday, and today, and for ever' (Heb. 13: 7,8). Does our evangelism present an unchanging Christ, both in what we say about Him and the way we say it? And if someone followed us for a week would they find the true unchanging Christ of glory, or our idea and our image?

Paul exhorted the Thessalonians in the last analysis, 'That ye would walk worthy of God, who hath called you unto his kingdom and glory' (1 Thess. 2:12). It will not be enough at the end of our evangelism to say, 'I did it my way.' We must evangelize His way and to the glory of God. Then the world will again have a God worth believing in and worshipping.

### Direction of the gospel

Before leaving this matter of the proclamation of the gospel, we need to realize that there is to be a God-given direction in both our preaching and witnessing, which too often appear irrelevant to the man in the street. How easy it is to preach not only above the heads, but also above the hearts of the people! Perhaps we have been at fault in leaving the whole matter of the application of our message to the work of the Holy Spirit alone. No doubt this is the Spirit's ministry, but does that remove from us the responsibility of speaking to the heart of the people and to the times in which we live? If our preaching is to be relevant today we must become like the men of Issachar who, we are told, 'were men that had understanding of the times, to know what Israel *ought* to do' (1 Chron. 12:32). We belong to a society which is becoming not merely immoral, but amoral. We belong to a church which has largely lost the ear of the people. At one end of the spectrum people base their opinions on the state of the world on *Letter from America* rather than on the Letter to the Romans; at the other they would rather worship at a Top-of-the Pops style meeting than the gospel meeting.

What has the New Testament to teach us in this matter? Quite simply that the church had a target at which they preached — the conscience or heart of the people. Paul said it all in describing the God-given direction of his preaching: 'But by manifestation of the truth commending ourselves *to every man's conscience* in the sight of God' (2 Cor. 4:2). We must define our terms before we go any further. Clearly, for Paul, 'manifesting the truth' was preaching, for he immediately informs us, 'We preach' (v.5). Similarly, for Paul, truth is definable; it is nothing less than the 'word of God' (v.2).

Finally, then, he preached the Word of God 'to every man's conscience in the sight of God'. Conscience is that 'something' to which every preacher preached and which every person possessed. It is that God-given faculty in every man that passes moral judgement on his actions, whether they be right or wrong, with the accompanying feeling of either pleasure or pain. The word properly means 'the moral judgement of the mind'. The mind, as we have clearly implied, sometimes approves its actions, while at other times it condemns them. What the great apostle Paul

realized was that the conscience of man needs the truth of
God. Clearly it is ignorant of God and requires to be taught
and enlightened by His Word; otherwise the judgement
and decisions it makes will be godless in character. It
becomes increasingly evident that, contrary to commonly
held opinion, every man possesses a conscience and that it
is possible for conscience to operate apart from any refer-
ence to God in its decision-making. That was clearly the
state of affairs in the society in which Paul evangelized and
surely it is also true today.

We should not be surprised that a famous pop star is
noted for saying, 'What I *think* is right is right.' For long
before him there were those in ancient times 'who did that
which was right in their own eyes'. Now, our brief is
evangelism — not psychology, sociology or philosophy.
Yet we must begin where people are, and not where we
want them to be. A sensible preacher is a man who sees
that preaching must have an aim: the ignorant conscience
of every man he meets. Yet though conscience is ignorant
of the Word of God, it is not ignorant of the word of
man. It is like a computer that has been programmed by
modern man, not by the eternal God. Unthinkingly it
produces the programmed responses: It 'doesn't believe
there is a God'; 'There are no absolutes'; 'There is no such
thing as right or wrong' (or, if there is, it is a matter for
each person, or for the group, to decide in each different
situation which confronts them). Evangelism is concerned
with enlightening the conscience of every man. The more
we study man in the Bible, we discover he has a conscience
which, though emphatic in what it believes, is often
emphatically wrong in its judgement, in God's estimation.
For example, taken at its worst extreme, a man can kill
someone and believe he is serving God! Alas! The history
of religion has often fulfilled Christ's prediction: 'Whosoever killeth you will *think* that he doeth God service'
(John 16:2).

Paul preached the Word of God to every man's conscience
because he remembered that he had once been both a
sincere persecutor and a blasphemer. Yet the root cause

was, as he tells us that 'I did it ignorantly in unbelief'
(1 Tim. 1:13). Beyond this, he followed his conscience
and did what he thought he ought to do. He testified to a
king, 'I verily thought with myself, that I ought to do
many things contrary to the name of Jesus of Nazareth.
Which thing I also did in Jerusalem: and many of the saints
did I shut up in prison, having received authority from the
chief priests; and when they were put to death, I gave my
voice against them' (Acts 26:9,10). Paul's memory of his
sincere but sin-darkened conscience prevented him from
despairing of King Agrippa, who thought the resurrection
was too incredible to believe. Paul reveals that a true understanding of the conscience is essential for true evangelism.
He sets us an example of this as he reasons with the king:
'Why should it be thought a thing incredible with you, that
God should raise the dead? I verily thought with myself,
that I ought to do many things contrary to the name of
Jesus of Nazareth' (Acts 26:8,9). We need the enlightened
conscience to address the unenlightened. Paul never forgot
in his preaching that the preparatory work of evangelism
was the preaching of the law of God.

In his Epistle to the Romans he shows not only that the
Jews are sinners, having disobeyed the law of God committed to them by Moses, but that the Gentiles are equally
guilty, having disobeyed the moral law of God written in
their consciences. His powerful reasoning reveals that men
who have not received the oracles of God are still under
the moral law of God. He argues, 'For when the Gentiles,
which have not the law, do *by nature* the things contained
in the law, these, having not the law, are a law unto themselves' (Rom. 2:14). He proceeds to show the evidence that
this is so: they 'shew the work of the law written in their
hearts, their conscience also bearing witness, and their
thoughts the mean while accusing or else excusing one
another' (v.15). The cutting edge of evangelism is the
preaching of the law of God to the conscience of man. It
is the law of God which cuts man to the quick. It wounds
him and makes way for the healing balm of the gospel. We
have a society which is almost totally ignorant of law

preaching in evangelism. For this reason 'there is no fear of God before their eyes'. Only when we preach the law of God will we again find the mouth of modern man silenced and the whole world guilty before God. How much we modern Christians need to 'know that what things soever the law saith, it saith to them that are under the law; that every mouth may be stopped, and all the world may become guilty before God'! (Rom. 3:19.)

We have today a society that has no conception of sin, 'having their conscience seared with a hot iron' (1 Tim. 4:2), and thus rendered largely insensible to God. This state of affairs, which characterizes the latter times of the world, was foretold by the Holy Spirit (1 Tim. 4:1). Yet we may take heart from the fact that a man who has lived for years without any consciousness of being a sinner can not only be converted but also changed into one of the greatest Christians and preachers that the world has ever known. He has helpfully left to this generation his personal testimony. He declares, 'For I was . . . without the law once.' He says at that time he had never heard the demands of God's holy law upon his sinful life, simply because 'without the law sin was dead'. Then there came a day in his life when for the first time he heard the claims of God's commandments. A most amazing reaction took place. Sin, which clearly had remained dormant in his life for years, came to life. He has to admit, 'When the commandment came, sin revived, and I died.' From then on his life was not worth living. Through the holy, just and good commandment of God, sin appeared in its true colours, 'exceeding sinful'. He was further forced to realize that such sin was dwelling in his very life. He made a final desperate attempt to adopt a good standard of living. But he was forced to admit, hopelessly, 'The good that I would I do not: but the evil which I would not, that I do.' In the midst of this terrible battle within he was driven to recognize himself as 'a wretched man' and thankfully found in the Lord Jesus Christ deliverance from the condemnation of the preaching of the law of God in his conscience (see Rom. 7:1 — 8:1).

There is still a further need of preaching directed to the

conscience, because the conscience needs, not only to be enlightened by the Word of God, but to be cleansed by the blood of Christ. It is an amazing truth to grasp that the Lord Jesus Christ directed His death towards the conscience of sinful man. God died for our consciences! The writer to the Hebrews, having declared the total ineffectiveness of the blood sacrifices of animals offered under the old covenant to do more than grant external and ceremonial cleansing, rises to the climax of his argument by declaring, 'How much more shall the blood of Christ, who through the eternal Spirit offered Himself without spot to God, *purge your conscience* from dead works to serve the living God?' (Heb. 9:14.) The power of sin is revealed not so much by the depth of defilement as by the depth of deliverance. Nothing less than the blood of Christ can cleanse the conscience in order that it can truly function again. The conscience 'being weak is defiled' (1 Cor. 8:7), and because of that defilement it is 'an evil conscience' (Heb. 10:22). The purpose of God-directed preaching is the same as the direction of the blood of God's Son, 'to cleanse the conscience from dead works to serve the living God'. Until the blood of Christ is applied to our consciences, our works are in character with our natures which are 'dead in trespasses and sins' (Eph. 2:1). We come to see that preaching of the law and gospel of God which is directed to the conscience will create not merely cleansed sinners, but a new society of those who will serve the living God. Surely this is the greatest need of our society.

The alternative for man is fearful indeed. It is to realize that 'there is a way that seemeth right unto a man, but the end thereof are the ways of death' (Prov. 16:25). May the direction of our preaching drive people from following their darkened, uncleansed consciences, from the precipice of destruction to the salvation of Christ.

# 5
# God-given direction

## A God-directed man

We must now fulfil our promise and return to the ministry of the evangelist Philip, and in particular to the way the Lord directed him to a new sphere of evangelism.

We see firstly how God directed him to *the area of his work*. He actually used one of His angels for this purpose. We read, 'The angel of the Lord spake unto Philip, saying, Arise, and go toward the south unto the way that goeth down from Jerusalem unto Gaza, which is desert' (Acts 8:26). We learn from this that Philip did not select his new sphere of evangelism; God did. God commanded him to move, from a place where his ministry was being greatly blessed, to seemingly nothing; humanly speaking it seemed both the wrong time to move and indeed the wrong place to which to move. Often human opinion must bow to divine direction before true evangelism can begin. Surely, this teaches us that even the greatest evangelist is not indispensable to God. Philip was merely the instrument of Samaria's blessing, but God was the source. But the most important truth to grasp here is that a God-directed man will go anywhere for God — even to a desert track, to a veritable 'B class' road! Today we have a host of 'A class' and 'motorway' evangelists, but few who dare to depart from the known route and pioneer a new track into the unknown for God. The spirit of Livingstone may, alas, be dead, but not the God of Livingstone.

We must be sure, as Philip was, of God's direction to our work, for only when we obey God's command to go will we, secondly, discover the God-given direction to *the person* (in this case) *we are to evangelize.* Philip did not answer God with the usual evangelical 'excuse': 'I must pray about it.' He knew that there is only one thing to do with a command of God, and that is to obey it. He did not ask for more time, for God's command meant to him that the time had come! This dramatic moment of pioneer evangelism brings together in one sentence the evangelist, the evangelized and the sending God: 'Arise, go toward the south' said God. Philip 'arose and went' and then (and only then) he saw an Ethiopian. If he had remained disobedient in Samaria, he would never have seen the treasurer to Candace, the Queen of the Ethiopians — let alone have led him to God. I shall always remember reading, on a burning hot beach in Italy, William Chalmers Burns's curt but courageous answer to the Presbyterian Missionary Board who asked him when he would be ready to leave for China. 'Tomorrow,' came back the answer, like an arrow from the bow of Burns. But then Burns, like Philip, knew what it was to be 'a polished shaft in God's quiver', ready to be taken by holy fingers and fired to the target of the human heart, however far away.

## A God-prepared place

We follow the southward movement of this desert-directed evangelist to the very spot where a missionary movement was to be inaugurated. At last the track was reached. Was there ever a more insignificant spot which had such significant consequences for God and man? God spoke again, not this time by an angel, but the voice of the Holy Spirit in the words: 'Go near, and join thyself to this chariot.' We believe that every event in this evangelistic drama had been directed from eternity by the Evangelist-in-Chief. Surely this was the beginning of the outworking of the prophecy: 'Ethiopia shall soon stretch out her hands unto God' (Ps. 68:31). To his amazement the first thing Philip heard was an African of great authority reading the Scriptures! Surely, Philip can hardly have believed his ears! But the Spirit of God who had sped him to that vehicle of state *en route* for Ethiopia placed on his lips the most important question he could ask the unsaved: 'Understandest thou what thou readest?' Philip knew, of course, that the man was reading the prophecy of Isaiah, but his real concern was whether he understood its message of salvation.

The historian Luke does not tell us how the Word of God came into the Ethiopian's hand. We do know, however, that God had directed that Ethiopian to the Scriptures as clearly as he directed Philip to the Ethiopian. Some time before this, a translation of the Hebrew Scriptures into Greek had been made by seventy great men at Alexandria and no doubt one of these copies had fallen into his hands. Under the direction of the Holy Spirit, this God-given principle and plan of evangelism bring together in one place, at one moment in history, two men who will become a vital part of church and world history: a Jew and an African; one the evangelist, the other to be evangelized in order to evangelize Ethiopia; two men from different worlds made one by God through the Word of God. Perfect direction led Philip to the right man, at the right time, at the right 'place of the Scripture' (v.32). How blind is unbelief! The Ethiopian discerns only the prophet who has written the portion of Scripture, but not the Saviour's suffering and death foretold by the passage. It is now that the purpose of Philip's desert mission is revealed. Much later a man of God said it all: 'How then shall they call on him in whom they have not believed? And how shall they believe in him of whom they have not heard? And how shall they hear without a preacher? And how shall they preach, except they be sent?' (Rom. 10:14,15.)

## A God-converted man

Philip knew his moment had come. He began at the Scripture which the Ethiopian could not understand. We must start at the point where people are, and not where we want to bring them. For 'Philip opened his mouth, and began at the same scripture, and preached unto him Jesus'. As the chariot moved towards Ethiopia, the Chancellor of the

Exchequer was becoming in a spiritual sense the richest man in the world, for he was discovering that in Christ are hid all the treasures of wisdom and knowledge. Suddenly, as the chariot was passing a desert watering spot, the Ethiopian in his turn asked a question. He wanted to know what stood in the way of his baptism. There and then, he wanted publicly to declare his new God-given faith. Philip, assured of the Ethiopian's whole-hearted faith in Christ, not only as the Saviour, but as God's Son, baptized him then and there. The mission was completed, but in another sense it had only just begun. The Spirit of God who directed Philip now as quickly removed him from the man he was never to meet again in this world. The stage was now filled by only one man — a new man in the same chariot, travelling to the same country, but with a new purpose. The joy of God travelled across the desert towards Ethiopia for 'he went on his way rejoicing'. Philip, too, was soon home. Mission accomplished!

How wonderful it is to prove that the God who directed first-century evangelists is the same God who directs those in the twentieth century. This was brought home to me powerfully one night as we were about to embark on our weekly outreach into the city. As I mentally viewed the city I felt burdened to pray, 'Lord, there are a lot of people out there tonight. Wilt Thou lead us as clearly as Thou didst lead Philip to the Ethiopian?' Later, as we climbed up high into a tower block and rang the first bell, the door opened — and there stood an Ethiopian! What an unforgettable night that was, as I and a fellow elder sat on his mat, telling him of a mighty Saviour who had literally led us to him out of all the other three hundred and twenty thousand city dwellers! I can honestly say that in my two-and-a-half year stay in that city I had never seen an Ethiopian before — nor, for that matter, since. Surely God gives us all such proofs from time to time to reassure us that we may expect God-given direction in His work of evangelism as specifically, and sometimes as dramatically as in New Testament times.

## A God-given directive

However, this particular illustration of divine direction in evangelism must be seen against the backcloth of a more general directive, namely, the great commission of Christ to preach the gospel to 'all nations' and to every creature until the end of time (Matt. 28:19, 20; Mark 16:15). In the last analysis this is the church's only objective authority for world evangelism – the Word of God, whereas, as we have seen with Philip, the subjective direction is by the Spirit of God. These powerful God-given constraints are never to be set in opposition to one another but are rather to combine for the evangelization of the world. Together they give the church both the authority and the constraint to evangelize.

But God has also given the church a more particular directive or plan of evangelism, which sets it in a geographical or global context. This was a later, more detailed plan delivered by Christ to His apostles during the six weeks of His life on earth after the resurrection. It was a command to be eyewitnesses of His death and powerful resurrection life, beginning at Jerusalem, their own city, then reaching out into the unevangelized region of Samaria, and then onwards 'unto the uttermost part of the earth' (Acts 1:8). Too often this magnificent vision of Christ has been set forth merely as an empowering for service, rather than as a directive to service. Indeed, when we see Christ's commission as His particular plan of evangelism for His church, we realize that the book of the Acts of the Apostles is nothing less than the acting out of that plan – a plan of which we today are still very much a part.

Yet Christ's blueprint for evangelism would have remained at the divine drawing-board stage if God had not also promised to provide His power to perform His plan. He twice promised to endue the disciples with spiritual power from on high (Luke 24:49 and Acts 1:8). In return He required that His church should both witness to and wait for that power (Acts 1:4,8). At least one hundred and twenty men and women met in an upper storey of a house in Jerusalem and for ten days they did nothing else but

pray over that divine blueprint and wait for further divine
developments.

They did not have long to wait, for there, in the very
place where Christ had promised, in Jerusalem, the evangelization of the earth began. In a sense world-mission was
born that day. For, through the Word of God preached in
the power of the Holy Spirit, 'men out of every nation
under heaven' heard the wonderful works of God. As both
the suffering of Christ and the power of the risen Lord
were portrayed before their eyes, men of every nation
cried out to know this Saviour. What an amazing sight it
must have been later as those thousands of people streamed
out of the city, carrying back to their distant lands upon
their camels not only new men of God, but a new God and
a new gospel! Behind them stood no longer merely the
familiar dome of the Jewish temple, but a new temple —
the church of God at Jerusalem consisting of new living
stones being built up into a spiritual temple.

The next great event of any consequence in the divine
direction of God's church in evangelistic outreach was the
outbreak of great persecution against it. Far from thwart-
ing the onward march of the church of God, this proved to
be the very force to drive the Christians into a new field of
evangelism. The historian Luke in his annals records for
posterity: 'And at that time there was a great persecution
against the church which was at Jerusalem; and they were
all scattered abroad throughout the regions of Judaea and
Samaria, except the apostles' (Acts 8:1). Far from frustrat-
ing God's plan for the evangelization of the world persecution fulfilled it, by initiating the next stage of evangelism
beyond Jerusalem, into Judaea and Samaria. (See Acts
1:8; 11:19.) Amazing as it may seem, the power of the
Spirit behind the evangelizing church and the power of
persecution confronting them were both instrumental
forces in the hand of God in the divine direction of evangelism. We have already seen how the Holy Spirit led an
itinerant evangelist beyond even Samaria to an Ethiopian,
and so began the outreach 'unto the uttermost part of the
earth'.

## A God-given corrective

In the case of Peter we are given the salutary reminder that these evangelists and apostles were, after all, men with traditional, and particularly nationalistic prejudices. For a period of time Peter was influenced more by his Jewish outlook than by the world vision of Christ to save men of all nationalities (Matt. 28:19,20; Mark 16:15; Acts 1:8). However, Christ was concerned that one biased man should not stand in the way of the work of God, and He enlarged Peter's vision of lost sinners other than Jews by a combination of particular directives.

As on many occasions before and since, it was in the place of prayer that God opened the eyes of His servant (Acts 10:9). While Peter was in that spiritually receptive condition, God staggered him by setting before him in a heavenly vision a meal of wild animals, reptiles and birds to be killed and eaten. So slow was Peter to swallow his deep-seated prejudice that God had to drop the tablecloth with its weird meal three times before the apostle's incredulous eyes. Peter had been slow to learn before. He, who had three times denied his Lord, had to be questioned three times by the risen Lord before being reinstated as an apostle of God. Finally, the vision 'died' before Peter's eyes and he sat bemused, doubting the meaning of it.

Suddenly his contemplations were interrupted by the voice of the Holy Spirit telling him that three men were at that moment approaching his house and that he must accompany them because they were sent by God. Confronted by these men, the impetuous Peter had to question them concerning the purpose of their coming. For Peter, as he listened to their story, truth was stranger than fiction. The men, he discovered, were the servants of someone called Cornelius, a military commander of some Italian regiment, a man of just character and also a man of prayer. He learned that this man was highly esteemed by the Jews, even though he was of another nation, and that God, through the instrumentality of an angel, had instructed him to send these men to Peter's door. Peter had no alternative but to accompany them.

That journey of about thirty miles, from Joppa to Caesarea, the centurion's home, proved to be one of the most important journeys Peter ever took. No doubt he considered not only the amazing happenings of the last few days, but in a sense, his whole life. Time and time again he must have asked himself, 'What is God trying to teach me?' We believe God gave him the answer because for Peter that coast road was also the way of obedience and he learnt a lesson that day which he never forgot. He had forgotten the teaching which, as a child, he had received from the Old Testament that God was going to send a Messiah, a Saviour, who would be a spiritual light to the Gentiles (Isa. 49:6). Had he also forgotten that great commission of Christ after His resurrection, given to him and the rest of the apostles, to preach the gospel to all nations, to every creature until the end of time? Had he forgotten the last words he had ever heard Christ speak: 'the uttermost part of the earth'? No preacher or writer can ever convey the death-blow which God was dealing out to Peter's nationalistic pride while, at the same time, opening his eyes to the world-wide evangelistic vision of Christ.

Little more needs to be said. Arriving at Caesarea Peter quickly insisted that Cornelius get up off his knees and listen as he confessed how throughout his lifetime he had been prevented by Jewish legalism from having any dealings with people of any other nation, lest he be contaminated by contact with them. He went on to relate God's dealings with him, leading to that moment of truth when he realized that he must see the whole of mankind as God does, without partiality and on an absolutely equal standing. In a word, 'God is no respecter of persons', God is no spiritual snob!

This was a moment of as great historical significance to Peter and to the church in succeeding generations as was Pentecost. For at this moment Peter began to preach to the Gentiles as powerfully as he had done at Pentecost, yet he preached a fuller gospel because he saw now that Christ was 'Lord of all'. This was the second Pentecost, that of the Gentiles. As Peter lifted up the crucified and risen Lord before the eyes of these Gentiles, God poured out the Holy Spirit upon them to the amazement of the Jews who had accompanied Peter. The apostles and other Christians situated in Judaea were bound to acknowledge this fuller direction of God in evangelism and rightly judged that the Gentiles, too, had received the Word of God.

Peter soon had to give an explanation of this first mission to the Gentiles to the questioning Jews of Jerusalem, who sat where, until recently, he had sat, in judgement upon all other nations. Peter rehearsed to them God's dealings with him up to the point of the descent of the Spirit of God upon him as he preached in Cornelius's house. He had, he said, suddenly remembered Christ's words to them before His ascension: 'John indeed baptized with water, but ye shall be baptized with the Holy Ghost . . .' He then realized that God had given to the Gentiles 'the like gift' and had to confess, 'What was I that I could withstand God?' The Jews could no longer doubt, but 'glorified God, saying, then hath God also to the Gentiles granted repentance unto life' (Acts 11:16,18). This incident provides a salutary warning for God's church in every age, showing the fearful danger of one man's narrow-minded vision limiting God's vision of the lost world.

This account once again reminds us that God has the right man for His work in a particular field. We also learn that He does not always use the obvious person. For, just prior to this, Philip the evangelist had returned to Caesarea, his home town, from evangelizing someone of another nation! Surely, we might say, here was the ideal man for winning Cornelius! But the God who often 'works in a mysterious way, His wonders to perform', has initially to teach the evangelist as well as those he is sent to evangelize, 'that no flesh should glory in His presence'.

This is a most appropriate point at which to trace the steps of the Christians who were dispersed by persecution at the time of Stephen's martyrdom. They were directed by God, not only northwards from Jerusalem a few hundred miles to Antioch in Syria, but even further to evangelize two of the Mediterranean islands, Cyprus and Crete (Acts 11:19).

## A God-given missionary policy

The church of God at Antioch now became the centre of evangelism following the preaching of the Word of God to the Grecians there. Barnabas was sent from the church at Jerusalem to examine their spiritual growth and, shortly after this, he encouraged Saul to come to teach God's Word for a year to these people, who were cleaving to the Lord with great purpose of heart. Without an understanding of these events, we would remain ignorant of God's preparation of a church which was to initiate three great evangelistic pioneer movements into the then known world. Here, most appropriately, God's people were first called 'Christians', and this church was marked out by God to be the initiator of the first church-based mission to the world.

It is vital to see how God directs a local church to evangelize. We see that He first reveals Himself to the leaders of His church while they are open to His direction in the acts of prayer and fasting. To a church spiritually attuned to God, God specifically named both the men He had called by instructing the church to 'separate me Barnabas and Saul for the work whereunto I have called them' (Acts 13:2). True church-based evangelism begins only when God directs and when the church is spiritual enough to discern that direction in sending God's chosen men to His chosen work. So united were the sending God and the sending church that the sending out of Barnabas and Saul is attributed equally to the church and to the Holy Spirit (Acts 13:3,4).

Second, we believe that Cyprus was chosen as the first virgin soil to be broken by God's messengers because God had already prepared the way for the evangelization of the island through sending the persecuted believers from Jerusalem there (Acts 11:19). Also, Barnabas as a Cypriot had, no doubt, both a knowledge of the people and a burden for them. In addition to this he had shown a truly sacrificial spirit in selling his land in his homeland (Acts 4:36). For Saul it was his first period of preparation for being the apostle to the Gentile, or heathen world. It is not

our purpose to lose ourselves in the detail of the first of
these four great church-based pioneer missions into heathen
Asia and Europe, but rather to see this simply as the logical
spiritual outcome of the mission empowered by Christ and
still going on into the uttermost part of the earth.

God directed His first evangelistic mission to the heathen
world mainly into cities, centring the preaching of the
Word of God on the Jewish synagogues. Their first mission
accomplished, the evangelists returned to their sending
church and reported back on the work (Acts 14:27). How
the church of Antioch must have thrilled as these New
Testament preachers rehearsed and recorded for posterity
'what God hath done'! Divinely directed men will always
record divine things. Yet in their report to their home church
human instrumentality was not ignored, let alone despised.
They acknowledged what 'God had done with them'. But
most significantly of all they attributed the pioneering and
opening up of the new mission field to God alone. It was
God whose hand had 'opened the door of faith to the
Gentiles' (Acts 14:27). At the same time, the task had been
hard and costly. John Mark had early proved to be the first
casualty in missionary work when he turned back, though
happily this was not the end of the story. The first great
mission of God to man met with faith and fury, love and
hatred.

This outreach had proved to be a mission with a difference
by becoming the first attack on the Gentile world. In a
sense, what had set out to be a Jewish mission had developed
into a Gentile or world-wide mission. It was a prototype of
all true missions to come. This must not be seen as in any
way a policy change in God's plan for world evangelization.
The turning away from preaching to the Jews (for a season)
and the turning to the Gentiles were by the outworking of
the world mission and plan of God to take the gospel to
every creature (see Acts 13:46,47). These first preachers
could only respond, 'For so hath the Lord commanded us,
saying, I have set thee to be a light to the Gentiles, that
thou shouldest be for salvation unto the ends of earth.'
This new evangelistic expansion gladdened the hearts of

the Gentiles and drove them both to glorify the Word of God and to receive it by faith (Acts 13:48).

God now directed these returning preachers to a time, no doubt, of rest and fellowship with their sending church at Antioch where 'they abode a long time with the disciples'. Deputation tours clearly took second place to the fellowship of the local church in New Testament times! The evangelists did, however, later embark on their first deputation meetings, touring the churches 'declaring the conversion of the Gentiles'. They were received with open arms and joyful response.

Finally, they travelled up to the city of Jerusalem and 'declared all things God had done with them' to the eager ears of elders and apostles. What followed was the honest airing of the difficulties arising from a new mission to a world of different culture, customs and traditions. Armed with a most clear and helpful directive, they returned again to their church at Antioch to await divine direction for the next mission.

Before embarking upon a second mission, they revisited or followed up every city where they had preached the Word of God (Acts 15:36). Their purpose was both specific and clear, namely, to 'see how they do' and 'confirming [literally, establishing] the churches' (Acts 15:41; 16:5). Yet we must not try to hide the fact that these early evangelists, being men, had their differences. At this particular juncture in the expansion of the work of God, Paul was not willing to give John Mark a second opportunity to prove himself, whereas Barnabas was. This resulted in Barnabas's taking John Mark with him for further evangelistic work on his island of Cyprus, whereas Paul, accompanied by Silas, retraced his former steps through Syria and Cilicia to Derbe and Lystra.

In our true understanding of the God-given principle of direction, it is vital to see that God directs His evangelists by the restraining and constraining influence of the Holy Spirit. In modern terminology, He both opens and shuts doors of evangelistic opportunity. This was especially the case as Paul, Silas and their new recruit Timothy were

about to break new ground, having covered the territory of
their first mission. Here we see that genuine human desire
to open up a new field must bow to divine direction. First
they 'were forbidden of the Holy Ghost to preach the Word
in Asia' (Acts 16:6). No doubt somewhat confused, they
pressed on with definite and decided plans for the evangelization of Bithynia, only to be restrained again by God.
The great apostle and evangelist, Paul, had to learn that even
he was not indispensable to God. Clearly he was not God's
man for Bithynia, nor was it God's time to open the door
for the evangelization of this place. It is, however, thrilling
to know that God had His man and His moment to work. In
112 A.D. Pliny, the Governor of Bithynia, writing to the
Roman Emperor Trajan could say, 'That the cause of the
Christians was a matter worthy of deliberation by reason
of the multitudes who were concerned, for many of each
sex, of every age, and quality, were and must be called in
question. This superstition having infected and overrun not
the city only, towns and countries, the temples and sacrifices
being generally forsaken.' No, Paul had nothing to worry
about as God closed the door for another day, for nothing
would change God's plan nor time for winning Bithynia to
God. How wonderful to know this God of evangelism is
still our God, and our responsibility is to be where God
wants us to be!

Paul clearly learnt his lesson, for he passed by Mysia
without attempting to cross its border to preach. At last
though, by both the constraints and restraints of God, the
second evangelistic mission came to a halt at Troas. There
was nowhere to go. Forbidden to go back, they found the
way forward barred by the blue Aegean sea. It was an
incident in some ways similar to that which confronted
Israel at the Red Sea. God alone could open up the way.
Paul and his companions now had to wait for God to work.

They did not have long to wait, for 'a man of Macedonia',
on the other side of the water, in Europe, appeared to him in
a God-given vision by night with the clear call to evangelize
by coming over to help them (Acts 16:9). To Paul the way
forward was plain, for behind the call of a man he discerned,

'The Lord had called us for to preach the gospel unto them' (Acts 16:10).

All these restraining and constraining directives led them, one unforgettable sabbath day, to a riverside prayer meeting made up entirely of women! Here we come to the climax in the God-given direction in evangelism. Where women prayed, God sent them a preacher, not just any preacher, but the greatest preacher in the world! He also sent them a sinner, not from nearby Philippi, but from the city of Thyatira. God could have converted her in the local church there (Rev. 2:18) but He had other plans. Here is the romance of the gospel: God led the women to pray for the preacher, and led the sinner to come 'whose heart the Lord opened, that she attended unto the things which were spoken of Paul' (Acts 16:14). The evangelization of Europe had begun with the first convert, and through two further missions it continued until, on his fourth and final mission, Paul reached Rome to stand before Caesar, but ultimately to stand before God to give account of the gospel he preached.

Such a consideration of the divine direction of the Acts of the Apostles in the evangelization of the then known world within about thirty years after Pentecost surely should drive us to ask ourselves, 'Do we experience similar direction?' Or rather, have we any biblical authority for saying God at a certain point of history will cease to direct His evangelizing church? We all know the answer to that question in our Bibles, but we must prove it in our own lives.

## A God-given change of direction

I reached a point early in my first ministry when I felt that nothing was happening (a very typical condition for all Christian workers). I felt led to spend a day with God and to pray for God to direct people to me. Space does not permit me to describe in detail the answer to that day of prayer. Suffice it to say that on the next day before I had breakfast a person was led to my manse in a fearful need. Some hours later, as that person was leaving, a second person came up my drive. The final contact was a man set on suicide who felt led to come to me and, mercifully, was saved by the grace of God. I say to my shame that often I have been blinded to God's divine direction through my own prayerlessness. There have been other times when I have felt I have known better than God. Once, I recall, as I was on my way to visit a person in hospital, a strong constraint came to me to turn off the road and visit a certain family. I drove on and reminded the Lord that I had been there only a day or two before. However, so great became the burden that I was forced to go back to that home and found that tragedy had come to the family since my last visit.

Every true Christian reading this book has also experienced, like Paul, the restraining hand of God. Our plans have been overruled by God's plans. I remember another night when I was convinced I should visit a certain lady, but was surprised to find her out. I drove away from her house, and stopping at a road junction, was preparing to turn when suddenly I felt restrained from doing so and at the same time constrained to visit the home of a young wife whose husband never came to church. Within moments of being shown into their lounge I was amazed to see the husband's eyes fill with tears as he asked, 'Could one come back to God?' That man had been an atheist for twelve years. He would not dare to enter his children's bedroom when his wife prayed with them at bedtime lest he contaminate them with his atheism. God made that man a Christian and a worker for God, through changing my plans that night. My whole point in narrating these works of God is to show that the God who directed first-century Christians is the same today if we will only prove Him and be taught by Him.

In case some feel these are rather exceptional ways of divine direction, I will close this chapter by recalling two other ways in which God directs His people. Firstly, by visiting the unconverted where one has been requested to do so. I believe the timing of such a visit may prove to be vital, even resulting in the conversion of the person concerned. I once was asked to visit a successful authoress by a friend of hers who was a Christian. That night I was in my study awaiting a visit from one of my church officers in about half an hour's time. I felt I must go and visit this woman. I literally ran through the night because I felt such a sense of urgency. I shall never forget her expression as she opened the door to me when I arrived. 'I was just trying to remember your name at that moment . . .' she let out. It transpired her work had suddenly come to an end. She had almost lost her sight suddenly, only a few days before she was due to appear on television. She moved her hand towards the manuscripts and paper lying over her desk. She told me she had lived for this. She was so dejected and at the end of her tether. She then told me how her grandfather, who had been a shepherd, had once taken her out to see his sheep and had then told her of the Good Shepherd and the lost sheep. All this had come back to her across the avenue of the years. She now knew what it was to be lost, but soon she was found. After I had prayed with her and pointed her back to the Saviour I ran rejoicing back to my study to keep my appointment. Within a few days that authoress kept an appointment, not at the television studios, but with her God and Saviour in heaven. How vital it is to be aware of God's timing!

Lastly, perhaps we need as churches and individual Christians to know that direction the apostle Paul knew for some three years in Ephesus when he could testify how he taught 'publicly and from house to house, testifying both to the Jews, and also to the Greeks, repentance toward God, and faith toward our Lord Jesus Christ' (Acts 20:20, 21). Here is a biblical example that has largely been ignored or forgotten. Paul knew not so much house-to-house visiting as house-to-house teaching or preaching. Rather than just inviting people to a meeting, he stressed there and then the need for repentance of sin and faith in Christ for the members of that household. We have often given up because we feel few come to church as a result. Some would even say, 'God will bring them; we don't need to go out to them.' Paul, however, saw house-to-house visitation as an opportunity of preaching the gospel just as much as in the synagogue or market-place. Though he longed to see souls saved, his final summing up of this work was not one of frustration and failure, but rather of another divine directive fulfilled. To every household he had visited in Ephesus he could declare, 'Wherefore I take you to record this day, that I am pure from the blood of all men. For I have not shunned to declare unto you all the counsel of God' (Acts 20:26,27). I wonder whether, as we drive through our villages, towns and cities we can hold up our hands and say, 'I am clear of your blood because I have preached the gospel to you, even in your homes.'

C.H. Spurgeon has always been a great encouragement to me in my ministry of evangelism. I count him as one of my best friends! I have been inspired, not only by his powerful preaching, but by his great concern for individual souls.

One day on regular door-to-door visitation I came to the home of a man who had prematurely gone blind. He was so appreciative of the visit that he encouraged me to call again. In the course of conversation, he told me about his secretary who was dying of cancer. Apparently her maiden name was Miss Spurgeon and her great faith in such adversity was challenging him at that time. He recounted that though Miss Spurgeon was married, for professional purposes she retained her maiden name because of a famous ancestor who was a great preacher. I could hardly sit still, let alone silent, as this dear man carried on the conversation. He told me that Miss Spurgeon used to recount a story how on one occasion her great relative before preaching in the Crystal Palace had wished to test how his voice would carry. He could not conclude the famous story because he was unable to recall what Spurgeon had said. My moment had come! I offered the words: 'Behold the Lamb of God that taketh away the sin of the world.' 'Yes, that's it, that's it', he responded. Then calling to his wife who was in the kitchen preparing tea he cried, 'My dear, Mr Bassett knows what Spurgeon said!' Like Philip with the Ethiopian, I was able to begin at that Scripture and that very afternoon led that dear man and, I believe, his wife, to the Lord. Later I had the joy of preaching from that text at his funeral. As I look up and see a family portrait of Charles Haddon Spurgeon on my study wall, I am forced to believe in a divine direction in evangelism which drives me to preach to sinners wherever God sends me.

# 6
# God-given vision

One of the greatest needs of the church today is to see the world as God sees it, through God's eyes and not our own. As long as we view it only through our naked eyes we will only see it naturally and not spiritually, and our solution to the world's plight will accordingly be merely human. The church should have a different solution to man's plight, because it has a different view of man. Vision is an essential requirement for the man of God, for as the proverb reminds us, 'Without a vision the people perish.' Where a world is perishing without the knowledge of God it is evidence of a short-sighted, if not blinded, church.

## Restored vision

The church has always required restored vision, and that vision has always come from the Redeemer Himself. We need to stand where Christ stood with His disciples long ago and see the mass of lost humanity through His eyes. It is recorded of Him: 'But when he saw the multitudes, he was moved with compassion . . .' (Matt. 9:36). We live in a statistically crazy world — a world which for years has numbered its soldiers rather than named them, and now reduces man to a number in the latest computer. The mass media also seek constantly, sincerely but ineffectively to convey the hunger of the world through impersonal sets of statistics. We have not only lost sight of the individual in the crowd, but he has been filed away out of sight as an impersonal fact or nonentity. We live in a world where matter is more important than a man and things more than people. In our age of the concrete jungle, and the high-rise block, we have, at best, a dehumanized man and at worst a soulless man whom one cannot grasp, let alone see or feel. I may perhaps be urged to care for his perishing body, but never, it would seem, for his immortal soul.

Though Christ's disciples viewed the same mass of lost and perishing humanity side-by-side with their Saviour it is recorded of him alone: 'When *he* saw the multitudes he was moved with compassion.' He clearly saw deeper than the physical. Spiritual eyes see beneath the surface and beyond the obvious. Spiritual vision sees beyond the seen. It also sees the many, but not at the cost of the one.

But although the disciples saw the same people as Christ, evidently they did not see the same plight that Christ saw. They had no sight of the soul condition of the people. It is not recorded of one of the disciples that he was moved with compassion. Until we see the world through Christ's eyes, we will never feel for it through Christ's heart.

## Spiritual blindness

From the disciples' spiritual blindness we learn that it is possible to be a minister of the gospel, an evangelist, a church officer, or worker in the church for year after year, and yet to have no vision of souls perishing in a world without Christ. So it is fearfully possible for our so-called evangelical churches to be going on with their business while the world just outside the door of the church goes unnoticed to hell. May God give us before it is too late the same vision He gave to His disciples when He commanded them, 'Say not ye, There are yet four months, and then cometh harvest? behold . . . lift up your eyes, and look on the fields; for they are white already to harvest' (John 4:35). Some members of the farming community say that when the corn is white it should have already been harvested. It is overripe! We have a world which is perishing in its sin because it is overripe for salvation. At the time of Christ's imperative command to evangelize, the church, as represented by His disciples, was standing back from evangelism because it believed the time was inappropriate. The time had not come!

It is good to recall the situation which prompted this God-given vision and command to 'put in the sickle' and evangelize. At the end of a long day Christ had wearily sat down on a well and sent away His disciples to buy food. In their absence Christ fell into conversation with a woman who had come to draw her water supply. Christ's eyes looked beyond the earthen waterpot she carried to her empty soul. Yet, remembering His thirst, He courteously asked her for a drink of water. Contact was made. Sympathy crossed the cultural barrier between Samaritan and Jew, man and woman. Christ did not debate the rights or wrongs of the centuries-old feud existing between their nations. Spiritual vision sees beyond nationalistic and cultural differences to the plight and need of a lost soul. It looks beyond the apparent need of an immoral woman to the true need of her soul, above all else to the solution — the living water of the Holy Spirit. A Man of such vision and such sympathy opened the sinner's eyes to Himself, to a Man more than a Jew, to more than a prophet, to the Messiah Himself. Leaving her empty vessel behind her she carried away a life which was no longer empty. Natural thirst had to wait because spiritual thirst had been met. She, too, now had spiritual vision. Rushing back to her village this formerly immoral woman wanted everyone to meet her new-found Saviour. Her invitation was fervent and personal: 'Come, see a man, which told me all things that ever I did: is not this the Christ?' (John 4:29.)

At this very time the disciples returned with the food for their hungry Master and were astonished to find He had lost His appetite, or rather exchanged it for a spiritual one. They could only believe someone else had brought Him food while they were away. Their problem was spiritual blindness. Having no spiritual vision of these lost Samaritans they could not understand Christ's insatiable appetite for the salvation of lost souls. Christ sought to show them their ignorance when He said, 'I have meat to eat that ye know not of.' He defined this evangelistic food for His soul as doing His Father's will and finishing His Father's work (John 4:34). Without spiritual vision of a lost world, the church will never know or have a spiritual appetite to win the lost, to do God's will, or to finish God's work for His Church.

Suddenly, at that point Christ evidently caught sight of a crowd streaming towards Him as a result of the Samaritan woman's witness, and pointed His disciples to them with the words: 'Behold . . . lift your eyes and look on the fields; for they are white already to harvest.'

How easy it is to be looking downwards, like the disciples, at our own lives or even at the legitimate matters within our churches, and to be blind to the streaming mass of humanity waiting to be saved. Yet we are told, 'Look not every man on his own things, but every man also on the things of others' (Phil. 2:4.) Have we forgotten the immortal words which follow: 'Let this mind be in *you*, which was also in Christ Jesus: who being in the form of God, thought it not robbery to be equal with God: but made himself of no reputation . . .'? Why, we may ask, was the Son of God willing to lay aside for a season the external emblems of His transcendent glory? The simple answer is because His heavenly vision of the lost drew Him down to the crib and ultimately to the cross.

The Word of God explicitly tells us that Christ had always had an eternal vision of lost humanity. In that tremendous eighth chapter of Proverbs we see Christ, who is the wisdom of God, represented by Wisdom and declaring in beautiful poetical language, 'When he appointed the foundations of the earth: then I was by him, as one brought up with him: and I was daily his delight, rejoicing always before him.' Then follow these amazing words: 'Rejoicing in the habitable parts of his earth; and my delights were with the sons of men' (Prov. 8:29,30). Incredible though it may seem, His vision was not of the rolling Atlantic, nor the glory of the Grand Canyon, nor the undulating desert of Arabia, but of those apparently insignificant specks which are lost mankind. However, to Christ, they were the most significant sight in the whole world. In His estimation, man is the only wonder worth His eternal vision and eternal care. It is for this reason alone that He came down the stairs of heaven and became 'obedient unto death, even the death of the cross'. This same vision must become the vision of the twentieth-century church even as it had to become that of the first-century church.

## Universal vision

Even a brief review of biblical and church history will reveal that no new outreach of the gospel has commenced without vision. Supremely, as we would expect, we find this is the case of God Himself. The first great judgement of the world and the salvation of the righteous minority was born out of God's own vision of the state of the world at that time. Moses graphically paints that momentous moment of the judgement of the world: 'And God saw that the wickedness of man was great in the earth, and that every imagination of the thoughts of his heart was only evil continually' (Gen. 6:5). We learn here that spiritual vision is total vision: total in scope, since it embraced within its vision the whole earth: and total in depth, for it focused also on the total depravity of the individual human heart. Godly vision always holds a universal vision, but not at the expense of seeing the individual in particular. So though God saw that 'the earth is filled with violence', and declared, 'I will destroy them with the earth', He never lost sight of Noah who 'found grace in the *eyes* of the Lord' (Gen. 6:8). Though it may rightly be argued that God's vision of the violence and the evil of man led to his destruction, it must never be forgotten that God waited one hundred and twenty years while Noah prepared an ark of salvation, and that for the same period of time Noah was a preacher of righteousness in that evangelistic mission which lasted for well over a century. For God was not willing that any should perish (Gen. 6:3; 2 Peter 2:5; 3:9).

Again, it was God's vision which initiated the deliverance of Israel from under the tyranny and thraldom of Pharaoh. It is wonderfully instructive, as well as comforting, to know that God has united His vision of His lost people with His covenant with those same people. The crack of the Egyptian taskmasters' whips did not deafen Him to the cry, or blind him to the plight of His people. The exodus was born out of God's vision: 'And God heard their groaning, and God remembered His covenant with Abraham, with Isaac, and with Jacob. And God *looked* upon the children of Israel, and God had respect unto them' (Exod. 2:24,25). That vision resulted in the calling and sending of an aged shepherd named Moses to become the saviour of God's people, centuries before God looked upon the world and saw His people under another tyranny and bondage prior to the incarnation. We read, 'And he saw that there was no man, and wondered that there was no intercessor' (Isa. 59:16). Though here God's vision was of His prayerless church in particular, His astonishment was that His people could be so blind and heartless, at a time when justice was standing afar off and truth was fallen in the street (Isa. 59:14). God's vision is so comprehensive that it embraces both the plight of a perishing world and that of a church blind to that world's need.

Even worse, the leaders of the church have often been unwilling to acknowledge the true state of the world. Such a man, orginally at least, was Jeremiah, for God commanded him to run through the streets of Jerusalem and review the spiritual and moral condition of the people. God's explicit command to His disbelieving prophet was: 'Run ye to and fro through the streets of Jerusalem, and see now and know, and seek in the broad places thereof, if ye can find a man, if there be any that executeth judgment, that seeketh the truth; and I will pardon it' (Jer. 5:1). Jeremiah was still unwilling to accept God's analysis of the situation. He even dared to argue that God was only looking on the lower and ignorant classes. He implied God's vision was partial and incomplete by his words: 'Surely these are poor; they are foolish; for they know not the way of the Lord, nor the judgment of their God' (Jer. 5:4). Jeremiah's philosophy was similar to that of those later Victorian philanthropists who saw education of the ignorant as the salvation of the masses. So sounded forth their social gospel. Yet even more spiritually-minded leaders have often directed the main thrust of their mission to the 'down-and-outs' and inner-city areas of our land. Jeremiah really believed 'the great' would respond to his preaching in a way the poor and foolish could not do. He blindly informed God, 'I will get me unto the great men, and will speak unto them; for they have known the way of the Lord, and the judgment of their God' (Jer. 5:5). Jeremiah's failure has often been the failure of God's church to see the *whole* world lying in the wicked one (1 John 5:19).

## Coke's vision

Lack of spiritual vision was surely the reason why the greatest missionary movement of the church was not really launched until the very close of the eighteenth century. At such a great moment of evangelical outreach we might well have expected that world vision of the lost to have proceeded from the heart of the dapper Oxford don whose heart God 'strangely warmed' in Aldersgate Street, London, in 1738. But John Wesley was not to be the father of modern missions. Indeed after this day's experience of the Spirit he did not venture forth again from Britain for nearly fifty years, centring his focus instead on the growth in personal holiness of his converts. But one of his lieutenants, Thomas Coke, a young Welshman, received such a God-given vision of the lost world that he produced a *Plan of the Society for the Establishment of Missions among the Heathen* in 1783. His plan was addressed and circulated 'to all lovers of mankind'.

It read:

The present institution is so agreeable to the finest feeling of piety and benevolence, that little need be added for its recommendation. The candid of every denomination (even those who are entirely unconnected with the Methodists, and are determined to be so) will acknowledge the amazing change which our preaching has wrought upon the ignorant and the uncivilized at least, throughout these nations; and they will admit, that the spirit of a missionary must be the most zealous, most devoted and self-denying

kind, nor is anything more required to constitute a missionary for the heathen nations than good sense, integrity, great
piety, and amazing zeal. Men possessing all these qualifications in a high degree, we have among us; and we doubt
not but some of these will accept of the arduous undertaking, not counting their lives dear, if they may but promote
the Kingdom of Christ and the present and eternal welfare
of their fellow creatures; and we trust nothing shall be
wanting, as far as time, strength and abilities will admit, to
give the fullest and highest satisfaction to the promoters of
the plan, on the part of your devoted servants,

THOMAS COKE

THOMAS PARKER

Thomas Coke was always regarded as the initiator of
this great plan of evangelism and Thomas Parker, a barrister
in law, as an able supporter. This plan, couched in rather
cold language, was hardly likely to convey the world vision
of the heathen which Coke no doubt hoped to express.
Later, however, he added an 'Address' which went some
way to communicate the needed vision. It announced, 'We
cannot but be sensible of the fallen state of Christendom
and the extensive room for labour which faithful ministers
may find in every country therein, but some of the nations
which are called Christian, are deeper sunk in ignorance
and impiety than others; and even in the most enlightened,
various parts are still buried in the grossest darkness.' It
was such language as this which challenged the Methodists
to overseas mission and earned Thomas Coke the honour
of being in a sense the father of Methodist missions. Yet
we have to wait another eight years before we find a
God-given vision of lost humanity set forth in a brief but
world-embracing enquiry into the true state of perishing
mankind.

## Carey's expectation

In 1786 William Carey, a young man in his early twenties,
recently called to a pastorate in the small Northamptonshire
village of Moulton, was to prove to be the man of vision

who would move the church to world mission. Barely man-
aging to exist, supplementing his meagre stipend with a
little shoemaking and school teaching, he nevertheless found
time to spend hours studying the globe of the world and,
among other books, the journals of the famous explorer
Captain Cook, who had died only a short time before.
Carey's eyes saw deeper than Cook's and to him fierce,
uncivilized cannibals were immortal souls for whom His
Saviour had bled and died. God also fired his vision with
the fuel of a little pamphlet carrying a wordy title customary
of the times, 'The Gospel Worthy of All Acceptation, or
the Obligations of men fully to credit and cordially to
approve whatever God made known. Wherein is considered
the nature of faith in Christ and the duty of all men where
the Gospel comes in that matter.' Andrew Fuller, the
author, was then unknown outside of his native Northamptonshire, yet he was to become nearly as famous as Carey
himself, and to be the God-given instrument to spur Carey
on to see that the gospel must be freely offered to all
people. Fuller himself had only recently been released
from a very narrow and limiting view of the offer of the
gospel. But now, like his Lord, he demanded in his pamphlet
that the gospel must be preached to every creature. Carey
drew this devastating and dramatic deduction: 'If it be the
duty of all men to believe the gospel . . . then it is the duty
of those who are entrusted with the gospel to endeavour to
make it known among all men.'

But now Carey's problems were only just beginning. His
greatest difficulty was to endeavour to make his discoveries
known, not initially to the lost and perishing nations of
the world, but to the visionless members of the church in
England! Little did that church at Moulton realize the full
significance of their charge to Carey 'to preach wherever
God in His providence might call him'! That charge was
given on 10 August 1786. A few weeks after Carey had
received it, he attended a ministers' fraternal in Northamp-
ton. Dr Ryland, who was chairing the meeting, sought to
encourage one of the younger ministers to bring up a matter
for discussion. Young Carey sprang to his feet and asked,

'Whether the command given to the apostles to teach all nations was not obligatory on all succeeding ministers to the end of the world, seeing that the accompanying promise was of equal extent?' It is difficult for us today to conceive how radical was the question, and how devastating must have been its influence upon the hearers. Carey did not have to wait long for his answer. Ryland clearly considered the whole matter preposterous, and said so in no uncertain terms. 'Young man' he began, 'sit down: when God pleases to convert the heathen, He will do it without your aid, or mine!' These words summarized the general blindness of Baptist leaders to world needs at the end of the eighteenth century. And yet this was a century which had seen a great spiritual revival and the evangelization of Britain on such a scale as had not been witnessed since Puritan times. Clearly the evangelization of the rest of the world was no matter of theirs!

A lesser man than Carey would have been crushed. But a man with God-given vision can neither be blinded nor silenced by man. World vision was now constantly the theme of Carey's sermons and the constant topic of his private conversation with his ministerial friends. Fuller himself was eventually won over to Carey's vision and went as far as to declare that the time had come to launch this world mission to the heathen. This was clearly the theme of a sermon preached at Clipstone at Easter 1791 upon the text: 'This people say, The time is not come, the time that the Lord's house should be built' (Hag. 1:2). There is no mistaking his meaning as he declared, 'The truth is that we wait for we know not what; we seem to think, "The time is not come, the time for the Spirit to be poured down from on high" . . ., we pray for the conversion of the world and yet we neglect the ordinary means by which it can be brought about. . . . How shall they hear without a preacher? And how shall they preach except they be sent?'

## Carey's Enquiry

By now Carey had become the minister of Harvey Lane

Chapel, Leicester. Here, fired with new support from
Fuller's sermon and further encouragement from his other
ministerial friends, he urged upon these friends the forma-
tion of a missionary society. As ever, they advocated
patience. One evening in Leicester, Carey read to them
from a manuscript he had begun in Moulton which put in
writing his burden and vision for world mission. Carey was
barely thirty years of age and yet his *Enquiry* was the result
of painstaking investigation into the state of every continent of the world. He went as far as to record the population
of every country and the religion of each. When we consider
how few records were available to him, we are amazed at
the authoritative testimonies which abound to the accuracy
of his records and figures. Minute details, such as the number
of inhabitants and the length and breadth of islands, are
concisely set out in an attempt to communicate his God-
given vision of the perishing world at large. The full title of
his manuscript was 'An enquiry into the obligations of
Christians to use means for the conversion of the heathen,
in which the religious nations of the world, the success of
former undertakings, and the practicability of further
undertakings, are considered by William Carey'. In his
eighty-seven page pamphlet, Carey traces God's great evangelistic movement through the church from Pentecost to
his own day. A reading of the *Enquiry* would no doubt go
a long way towards restoring lost vision to ministers and
members of God's church.

    Carey is remembered either for his immortal words:
'Expect great things from God, attempt great things for
God,' or his description of his approach to his work as a
missionary in India: 'I can plod.' Yet beside these must
surely be placed the final impassioned appeal of the *Enquiry:*
'"Whatsoever a man soweth that shall he also reap." What
treasure, what an harvest must await such characters as
Paul and Eliot and Brainerd! . . . What a heaven will it be
to see the many myriads of poor heathens, of Britons
among the rest, who by their labours have been brought to
the knowledge of God. Surely a crown of rejoicing like this
is worth aspiring to. Surely it is worth while to lay ourselves
out with all our might, in promoting the cause and Kingdom
of Christ.'

# 7
# God-given compassion

## The heart of God

Compassion, like vision, is something you cannot create. You cannot work it up. You have to go to the heart of God and to His Word and begin to see man through the eyes of God. A vision of the lost is the prerequisite for compassion for the lost. Compassion is born out of vision, and both must proceed from God. Christ is the exemplar of both, for of Him we read, 'But when He saw the multitudes, He was moved with compassion on them' (Matt. 9:36). The background to this moment of deep pathos is Christ moving through every city and village preaching the gospel. No place escaped His visitation. No one escaped His message. His strategy was not the result of some cold calculating plan for world evangelization, but of the movement of God's mercy for man. Here is nothing less than the heart of God moving towards lost man.

The word 'compassion' in the original means that Christ was moved to the depth of His being. It is the same Greek word as that used by Paul when speaking of Onesimus, the slave who had run away from his master Philemon — only to run straight into the arms of Paul in Rome! Paul, having had the joy of leading him to Christ, sends him back to Philemon with a view to his being received as a new person and in a new way. He therefore describes what he now feels for his new convert. Paul tells Philemon that he is 'mine own bowels' (Philem. 12), that is, as dear and as cherished as himself. To have compassion is to love sinners as much as you love yourself.

The same word is used again by the apostle Paul when
he is writing to the church at Philippi. Even though he is
now 'Paul the aged' he will never forget the day when, in
response to that vision in the night, the Macedonian call
for mercy, he moved from Asia to Europe. Eventually he
caught sight of the riverside, and of that group of godly
women who asked him to preach, just as the seller of purple
walked in — the first convert. Then there was that young
woman caught up in the occult, and the jailor who nearly
committed suicide in the jail at the time of the earthquake,
because he thought all the prisoners had escaped. What a
sight of pitiful trembling humanity he looked as he sprang
into the cell pleading to know the way of salvation! No
doubt as he wrote his Epistle from prison, Paul looked back
on these things and thought, 'I never could have done it
without being sent to Macedonia on that mission of mercy
and being constrained by Christ-given compassion.' He
paused for a moment to receive from God the right word
to express the depth of feeling he still possessed for those
believers in Philippi, now formed into a church. There could
only be one word to describe his feelings: the same word
which took him to Philippi in the first place — compassion!
God knew he was neither lying nor exaggerating. So his
pen hovered no longer over the parchment and he wrote,
'God is my record [my witness], how greatly I long after
you all in the bowels of Jesus Christ' (Phil. 1:8). What a
man! He can even call upon God Almighty to witness the
depth of his love for these Christians! Yet in the last analysis
it was not Paul's love to which God was called to bear
witness, but God's own love through Paul. Indeed it was
not Paul's natural love, for he takes us back to the source
of his compassion, 'the bowels of Jesus Christ'. Christ's
heart must capture our hearts before we will ever be
characterized by compassion for a lost world.

## The plight of man

We will, however, only begin to experience such Christ-like
compassion when we see the multitude and mass of lost
humanity as He did. As vision is to see man through God's

eyes, so compassion is to love the world with God's heart. Alas! How often we have made the mistake of trying to love the unlovely world with our own loveless hearts! Christ, as we have seen earlier, saw beyond the obvious and beneath the surface. Compassion sees the threefold cause of man's plight, yearns over it and moves to remedy it. Christ *saw* and *felt* something which the disciples failed to recognize.

Firstly, the multitude were 'fainting'. No doubt this was in a sense true physically, but even more essentially, spiritually. Sin has weakened men's very constitution. It has eaten away and eroded both his moral and spiritual fibre. Another word which describes the condition of mankind without God is 'prayerlessness'. We are reminded of Christ's maxim for man: 'Men ought always to pray and not to faint.' In His estimation the opposite to praying is not simply not praying, but fainting. For prayer is dependence upon God, prayerlessness is independence. A fainting world or a fainting individual is only a picture of a spiritually independent world weakened by sin.

Secondly, sin has also scattered mankind, not only from God, but also from one another. How incredible that a man, made in the likeness and image of God, should have been reduced to a mere animal — and a pathetic sheep at that: 'scattered abroad as sheep'! How has such a state of affairs come about? To discover its cause we need to go back to a great evangelical preacher living some seven hundred and fifty years before Christ. He describes the reason for man's being scattered. It is that 'all we like sheep have gone astray' (Isa. 53:6). 'But why?' we ask. We are left in no doubt of the answer: our wilfulness. 'We have turned every one to his own way.' We have stubbornly refused to go God's way. We have chosen to carve out our own destiny. We have become, to use another picture, a world of scattered islands on the sea of sin. As God views us through eyes of compassion, He does not see us as we see ourselves. He sees us, not as a homogeneous whole, not as related to one another, but cut off and alienated from one another and, above all, from Himself. It is only after we have become Christians that we realize that in God's sight we 'in time

past were not a people, but are now the people of God'.
The reason, the secret, is this: then we 'had not obtained
mercy, but now have obtained mercy' (1 Peter 2:10).

  Thirdly, Christ saw that the people were shepherdless. A
shepherdless flock will always wander. This was the
supreme reason why Christ came into this world — for a
shepherdless world and a shepherdless church. Only a man
who can truly say, 'The Lord is my Shepherd' will ever go
on to see, 'I shall not want.' The tragedy of our world is
that it does not know it has lost its Shepherd or that the
Good Shepherd laid down His life for the sheep. It is also a
fact that no New Testament church lacked an under-
shepherd, a God-given minister. We are categorically told
that the apostles appointed elders in every church (Acts
14:23), and the risen Christ's gift to the church is a pastor
and teacher (Eph. 4:11). A pastorless and shepherdless
church was an unknown entity in the New Testament. Let
us realize God's heart is moved to the depths over shepherdless congregations. May the same be true of our hearts! In
fact it is wonderfully moving to recognize that the gift of
the pastor or shepherd to each local church is a gift from
the heart of God. What a promise to us in our day: 'And I
will give you pastors according to mine heart, which shall
feed you with knowledge and understanding'! (Jer. 3:15.)

## The compassion of God

Yet if we are to rediscover and regain this lost passion for
souls we must confess our hardness and coldness of heart
to God. It is only then that we realize compassion is an
attribute of God. The picture of God in both Old and New
Testaments is of a God 'full of compassion'. We need to go
further and discover that the only reason for the continuing
existence of the world is the unfailing compassion of God.
This was the conclusion to which Jeremiah was driven as
he surveyed the desolation of Jerusalem and of the world
of his day. His own life was filled with bitterness, and he
declared in his misery that his 'hope is perished'. Then
suddenly into his utter hopelessness there broke in an

amazing ray of light: 'This I recall to my mind [Hebrew 'make to return to my heart'], therefore have I hope' he declared. 'It is of the Lord's mercies that we are not consumed, because *his compassions fail not*' (Lam. 3:21,22). How different is this view from that of modern man! He traces his own continuing existence and, indeed, that of the world, to the fact that no one has dared to 'push the button'. Rather than God's unfailing compassion, he believes it to be the fear of retaliation alone which keeps man from embarking upon the war to end all wars.

Jeremiah, however, even in the midst of his recorded lamentations, now has new heart, as he looks out upon the desolations of the same world. In the light of the unfailing compassion of God he now proves that every new day is to be met with new compassions from God. For he realizes, 'They are new every morning.' A new thing has dawned on this man of God: compassion is the only answer to a desolate and otherwise hopeless world. He is quick to acknowledge now that the daily provision of new compassion from God flows from the unfailing source of God's compassions. For only the man who has experienced the daily newness of God's unfailing compassion can testify, 'Great is Thy faithfulness' (Lam. 3:22,23). A compassionless world will not only be devoid of forgiveness to its fellow man or nation, but sometimes set on man's destruction and not his salvation.

If the church of the twentieth century fails to rediscover that there is an ocean of compassion daily to be found in God's heart, it will be as hopeless as was the preacher Jeremiah before he made his discovery. Before it is too late we, like the psalmist of old, must recognize, 'But he, being full of compassion, forgave their iniquity, and destroyed them not; yea, many a time turned he his anger away, and did not stir up all his wrath' (Ps. 78:38). We in the fearful times in which we live, need to pray to God, 'In wrath remember mercy.'

Yet having returned to the heart of God's compassion and stood in wonder and surely, worshipped, we must consider God's compassion in action. I have often told new

converts to read the Gospels as authentic biographies of
Christ and identify themselves with the people among
whom Christ moved daily. Yet I admit I have failed to
identify myself with Christ, especially in His compassionate
dealings with such people. Christ's life was compassion in
action. He is described as not only being filled with compassion, but moved by compassion. His compassion moved
Him towards man. He acted not out of duty, but out of
devotion. His soul yearned for their souls. From beginning
to end, from the leper to the dying thief, Christ's whole
ministry was exercised under the compulsion of compassion.
His outward plan of ministry was directed by the inner
power of mercy, and so must ours be.

Christ's compassion not only moved Him towards men,
but moved men towards Him. We read, for instance, that a
leper came to Christ: 'And there came a leper to him . . .
and kneeling down to him, and saying unto him, If thou
wilt, thou canst make me clean' (Mark 1:40). Christ's reputation had clearly gone before Him. Christ was known as a
Man worth approaching, as a God worth worshipping. The
leper kneeled not just with his knees, but clearly also with
his heart. He worshipped this God of compassion, and with
a God-given faith he realized that the cleansing of a soul
rests with the will of God. He neither doubted nor denied
Christ's power, or he would never have come. He put his
unclean life under the will of God.

We see from this passage that the salvation of a soul
begins with the movement of compassion. It was compassion that moved first the heart of God, then the hand
of God and finally the voice of God. The heart of compassion
moved and the hand of compassion broke through the
ceremonial law to touch the unclean sinner. The voice of
compassion commanded the cleansing of the sinner: 'Be
thou clean' (Mark 1:41). Yet, if we see this cleansed man
merely as the leper in Mark's Gospel, we miss the whole
point of Christ's recording this incident. The unclean are
still with us, though, sadly, more outside our churches
than within them. 'Why?' we may well ask. We know that
on the whole we are respectable, middle-class churches. But

is that really the answer? Is the truth not rather that the unclean sinner does not find us warm, compassionate and reaching out to him? He is often misunderstood and both unloved and unwanted. Yet though we believe that Christ was a man 'apart' in the sense He was 'holy, harmless, unde-filed and separate from sinners', unclean sinners sought Him. They knew He wanted to help them. They knew He had not only the will to help them, but the heart to do so.

When Christ became a man He refused to have the body of a superman, but took a body which was 'touched with a feeling of our infirmities'. His condescension reached not only to His manhood, but to His ministry. Have you ever realized that He allowed Himself, in a sense, to undergo the same selection system that every minister or high priest in Israel went through? No high priest ever was a self-appointed minister. The rule was both unbreakable and emphatic that 'no man taketh this honour unto himself, but he that is called of God, as was Aaron. So also Christ glori-fied not himself to be made an high priest . . .' (Heb. 5:4,5). Christ was ordained by God the Father with the words: 'Thou art my Son, today have I begotten thee.' He, too, like every other high priest submitted Himself to a further step in selection, namely that 'every high priest taken from among men is ordained *for men* in things pertaining to God . . .' (Heb. 5:1).

## The ministerial requirement

Christ, like every other minister in Israel, had to be of the right character for such a high office. We might well have expected a great academic degree in rabbinical knowledge would have been the basic requirement. Though, no doubt, the Jewish ministry was a learned ministry, yet heart know-ledge, not head knowledge, was the essential requirement for the ministry of God that even Christ as a high priest would have been required to possess. For the ministry must be able to meet the basic needs of man. The minister must be one 'who can have compassion on the ignorant, and on them that are out of the way' (Heb. 5:2) and in addition he must be a man 'compassed with infirmity'. This is why

God uses men, and not angels who have no feelings for the frailty of man. Though Christ was sinless, He still knew in His own body the infirmities of those around Him, apart from sin.

A ministry that is devoid of compassion will have no feeling for the lost mass of humanity, rendered ignorant of the knowledge of God by the Fall, nor will it follow lost man who has gone 'out of the way'. Only a man who is 'compassed with infirmity' and can 'sit where they sit' is equipped to be a preacher to such a world. If the Prince of preachers, the Lord Jesus Christ, was willing to be tested by such a standard, how much more must we be! Yet how often does our local church, Bible college or missionary board test the call of the man of God by the condition of his heart? Surely it is not too harsh to say that a compassionless heart invalidates any supposed call to the ministry. In the end it will be fairer not only to the candidate, but to the lost race of sinners not spoken to in their ignorance, nor sought in their waywardness.

With this in mind, let us pray for a new anointing of God-given compassion upon our churches. Then we will see again the unconverted coming into our services, and beside him we will see again another new man 'seated, clothed and in his right mind'. Remember, those words were spoken of the one of whom it was commonly said, 'Neither could any man tame him.' We pray for such a man to be converted in our prayer meetings, but why do we not see someone changed like that in our midst? Do you say, 'Because we need a revival first'? I wonder. When Christ converted this man he wanted to stay with Christ and go anywhere in the world to serve God. But Christ knew such a man had a message for his own home and his own neighbourhood. What, we may well ask, was that message Christ wanted his home town to know? 'Go home to thy friends, and tell them how great things the Lord hath done for thee.' Was that all? No, Christ added these words: 'And hath had compassion on thee' (Mark 5:19). Christ's compassion is contagious. In that place called Decapolis, though Christ had converted the biggest sinner in town and changed the worst citizen to the most respectable citizen, they pleaded with Him to 'depart from their coasts'. And yet, after he had gone, the devil-possessed man who had been won by compassion changed his community with that same Christ-given compassion! For, 'He departed, and began to publish in Decapolis how great things Jesus had done for him: and all men did marvel' (Mark 5:20). Let us each ask ourselves when we last saw in our community people who one moment did not want to have the presence of Christ among them, yet in the very next moment were filled with wonder at the same God. This can only happen when the power of Christ-given compassion conquers a community. Incidentally, Christ did return to Decapolis, where He had been asked to leave town, and the result was boundless astonishment. We read that the inhabitants 'were beyond measure astonished, saying, He hath done all things well . . .' (Mark 7:37).

Compassion is needed in dealing with all sinners, but the Scripture warrants our saying that it will be needed more and more by the individual Christian, minister and church of God, as we draw nearer to the end of the world. Jude reminds us of Christ's words: 'There should be mockers in the last time, who should walk after their own ungodly lusts' (Jude 18). In this coming sensual age he enforces on all believers the need to build themselves up, in the sense of fortifying themselves against such pressures, by praying more than ever and keeping their lives in the love of God. Clearly no monastic exclusive separatist movement is called for. To those who have gone astray, compassion is to be the hallmark of a church in a sensuous and increasingly ungodly society. Compassionate evangelism is to be the order of the day: 'And of some have compassion, making a difference' (Jude 22). Compassion will make a difference in that it distinguishes the particular sin and need of different individuals in society. Compassion not only feels for the ungodly, but fears the sins of the ungodly, as a fireman rescues the man from the burning house pulling him out as quickly as possible in case he is burnt. Our fear is of the fire of sin, so we are not only concerned to be 'pulling them out of the fire' motivated by Christ-given compassion, but at the same time 'hating even the garment spotted by the flesh'.

Compassion is seeking to save the sinner, and beholding his plight, but never at the cost of fearing the power and contagion of sin.

Finally, a compassionate man is a man who has God-given vision and compassion for the lost. To be such a man he needs to be so close to Christ in his life that he becomes one with Him in compassion. No greater example can be found of a man whose life, belief and conscience were controlled by Christ's compassion than the apostle Paul. He can declare, 'I say the truth in Christ, I lie not, my conscience also bearing me witness in the Holy Ghost, that I have great heaviness and continual sorrow in my heart. For I could wish that myself were accursed [separated] from Christ for my brethren, my kinsmen according to the flesh' (Rom. 9:1-3). He reminds us of Moses' degree of burden for lost Israel when he was willing to have his name taken out of the book of life that their names might be written there in his place (Exod. 32:32). So likewise Paul, who formerly hated these Jewish Christians and persecuted them unto death, has known the compassion of Christ replace the hatred of sin. He, too, is willing to be separated from Christ and accursed for ever if it will gain their salvation. Paul shows us the complete Christian, seemingly a paradox — rejoicing and sorrowing in the same heart at the same time. He, who could 'rejoice in the Lord always', could equally say, 'I have great heaviness and continual sorrow in my heart' over his lost people. God give us a like heart! Then it will be written: 'When *they* saw the multitude, *they* were moved with compassion.'

# 8
# God-given prayer

'Then saith he unto his disciples, the harvest truly is plenteous, but the labourers are few.'

## Prayer for workers

Firstly, we need a God-given burden of prayer for workers.
We are so moved by Christ's description of lost humanity
perishing before our once blinded eyes that, as we open
them to see the fields white already to harvest, we feel the
next step is obvious: it is to go and preach the gospel
immediately and recruit others to join us. Such is the
inspiration of Christ's vision of, and compassion for, the
lost, that we wait in eager expectation for the command to
go and preach. Yet the command never comes. Not, that is,
the command to preach to the lost, but the command to
pray: 'Pray ye therefore the Lord of the harvest, that he
will send forth labourers . . .' The reason for prayer is
because the number of souls waiting to be harvested far
outnumbers the labourers. For in Christ's estimation, 'the
harvest truly is plenteous, but the labourers are few'. How
pathetic, and yet how challenging, that the needy souls
waiting to be saved in our world far outnumber the
preachers and workers of the gospel! Yet prayer is needed
also because Christ alone has lordship over the harvest of
lost souls. What an encouragement to know that Christ is
Lord not only of the church, but also of the lost! He is
Lord of the harvest. For that reason alone we must pray to
Him. We have seen His lordship of vision and His lordship
of compassion, but we need also to see His lordship of
labour.

We are called to pray to the Lord for a very special person, for a very special work: for someone who possesses the Lord's vision and the Lord's compassion, who realizes at the outset of the work of evangelism that he is overwhelmingly outnumbered by the lost. The numerical statistics of the perishing world demand that a man appreciate that the magnitude of the task is such that, without Christ, it is beyond him. How can the few reach, let alone save, the many? Particularly when we realize that they are scattered by sin across the face of the earth and are fainting in their sins without a shepherd to help them. Did not Milton cry out, 'The hungry sheep look up and are not fed'? Are they not like the man by the Pool of Bethesda who for years on end had sat unnoticed, unloved and unreached? Christ was amazed he had not been saved before. The man's answer to Christ was a condemnation of the compassionless church: 'Sir, I have no man . . .' (John 5:7).

What Christ is saying is that we must pray that such a state of affairs may never exist again, when the lost are waiting for years on end to be saved, and no man has the time to bother about them.

It is interesting that Christ did not say the Christians are few, but the labourers are few. Often the Christians in our churches are many, but the labourers are few. We need not only to pray for more labourers, but surely that Christians will be changed by Christ into labourers among the lost. We are praying for a rare man, one who is a gift of God to the church. For, if the church could produce such men, Christ would not command us to pray for them. If Christ has promised them in answer to prayer, they will come. Yet only if we pray will evangelists and church members be sent to evangelize among the lost, young and old, of our villages, towns and cities. We need to pray for a new generation of pioneers. Is it not a case of 'Ye have not because ye ask not'? But, as vision comes before compassion, so prayer follows both. A visionless and compassionless church will not be praying for labourers. However, when we begin to pray, the grace of God will lay hold upon men who will do the work of ten men or more. Such was the testimony of Paul when he surveyed his labour for lost souls. He could trace the change the grace of God made not only in his life but in his work for God and man. For he wrote, 'I am the least of the apostles, that am not meet to be called an apostle, because I persecuted the church of God. But by the grace of God I am what I am; and His grace which was bestowed upon me was not in vain; but I laboured more abundantly than they all: yet not I, but the grace of God which was with me' (1 Cor. 15:9,10). In a sense his labours exceeded those of the rest of the disciples put together! He laboured across different continents for God, not merely in preaching and in prayer, but labouring from 'house to house' night and day.

Is there not a danger today that in our churches we are praying for part-time missionaries, ministers and workers on short-term service? When did we last hear a prayer for a labourer? Dare we pray, 'Send us another Paul, another Carey, another Studd'? I am frequently challenged by the picture on my study wall of an old bald-headed man in a bush jacket. He is no longer handsome, young or strong. He is 'burnt out for God'. His immortal words written beside his worn-out mortal body challenge me: 'If Jesus Christ be God and died for me, then no sacrifice can be too great for me to make for Him.' Such was the maxim of C.T. Studd.

Such men when they come from God will labour with Pauline zeal and like a woman giving birth. So Paul again can challenge us: 'But it is good to be zealously affected always in a good thing, and not only when I am present with you. My little children, of whom I travail in birth again until Christ be formed in you' (Gal. 4:18,19).

It seems abundantly plain that a prayerless church will not have labourers given it by God. God will trust only a prayerful church with labourers, because they will still require the prayers of the church even when God has given them back to the church. Surely we will never see a new generation of effective labourers until we see a new generation of men and women who pray effectively. We need those who, like Epaphras, will be 'always labouring fer-

vently for you in prayers' (Col. 4:12). Then again in evangelism we need labourers like Epaphroditus, who was Paul's
'companion in labour' and at the same time the 'messenger'
of the church at Philippi (Phil. 2:25). Supremely we have
the example of Christ Himself, who did not appoint the
apostles to evangelize the world until He had spent a whole
night praying for labourers. For we read of Him, 'And it
came to pass in those days, that he went out into a mountain to pray, and continued all night in prayer to God.' We
are left in no doubt of the purpose of His all-night prayer
vigil for 'when it was day, he called unto him his disciples:
and of them he chose twelve, whom also he named apostles'
(Luke 6:12,13). These were special men: they were 'the
prayed-for ones of God'; they were disciples, 'the taught
ones of God', who became the apostles, 'the sent ones of
God'. We, too, need to pray before we send men in God's
name.

Returning to Christ's command to the church to pray
the Lord of the harvest for labourers, we must add one
final cautionary word. If we would pray personally for
labourers it is implied that we must be willing to be one of
those labourers if God so chooses us. For Matthew 10 com-
mences, 'And when he had called unto him his twelve
disciples . . .' Clearly, if we call upon God for labourers,
we must be willing to be called by God to be a labourer for
the Lord of the harvest.

Why is it, we may well ask, that we give so little time to
prayer in proportion to other work we do for the Lord? Is
it not, in the last analysis, that in fact we do not equate
prayer with work? That great missionary, James Gilmour,
who laboured for God in Mongolia, came to this same conclusion: 'There is a great feeling that when a man is praying
he is doing nothing, and this feeling makes us give undue
importance to work, sometimes even to the hurrying over
or even to the neglect of prayer.' Another great missionary
labourer for God, Edward Payson, said it all when he
declared, 'If we would do much for God we must ask
much of God.'

Before leaving this graphic picture of the harvest field of

the world, we need to see that God revealed first the field
of labour and then called for prayer for workers. We need
to ask the Lord to show us, in our churches, where He
wants us to labour for God. How easy it is to draw up
plans of operation and areas of outreach, without first ask-
ing the Lord to show us His work! Perhaps there is no
greater prayer in this context than this one: 'Let thy work
appear unto thy servants' (Ps. 90:16). There follow four
further precious pithy petitions concerning that God-given
field of service: 'and thy glory unto their children,'; then,
'and let the beauty of the Lord our God be upon us'; and,
in conclusion, a repeated petition, 'and establish thou the
work of our hands upon us; yea, the work of our hands
establish thou it.'

What wonderful condescension of our God! When we,
His labourers, pray to Him He not only shows us the field
of work for Him, and allows His beauty to rest upon us,
but He puts His work into our hands. His work becomes
our work. Yet we must never labour independently of
God, for in answer to prayer He alone will grant us success
by establishing 'the work of our hands'.

## Prayer for power

Our praying work does not cease when we have prayed for
workers and for a field of labour. We need a God-given
burden of prayer for power. For Christ not only appointed
His witnesses to preach, and instructed them what to
preach, but He also commanded them, 'Tarry ye in the
city of Jerusalem, until ye be endued with power from on
high' (Luke 24:45-49). Again, He promised, 'But ye shall
receive power, after that the Holy Ghost is come upon
you: and ye shall be witnesses unto me' (Acts 1:8). The
God who commanded His people to 'tarry' also commanded
them to 'wait for the promise of the Father'. They inter-
preted this, not as a call to idle passivity, but to prayerful
activity. It was translated by the men and women of the
early church into a ten-day prayer meeting, pleading these
promises of God for a spiritual power from on high. How

often as we open the Acts of the Apostles we discover the early church at prayer! This most certainly is the case as we peer into the upper room in Jerusalem prior to the day of Pentecost and discover that 'these all continued with one accord in prayer and supplication, with the women' (Acts 1:14). They, like Jacob of old, prevailed in prayer for the power of God. Though we do not have their actual petitions recorded, they must have prayed in those days in similar terms to Jacob when he cried, 'I will not let thee go, except thou bless me.' Did they not, like Jacob, come to 'power with God and with men' because like him they 'prevailed'? (Genesis 32:26,28.) Not only revival is born out of prevailing prayer to God, but evangelism likewise. For Pentecost was but the birthplace of world mission. It was nothing less than the empowering of the church to evangelize the then known world. For we read, 'Parthians, and Medes, and Elamites, and the dwellers in Mesopotamia, and in Judaea, and Cappodocia, in Pontus, and Asia, Phrygia, and Pamphylia, in Egypt, and in the parts of Libya about Cyrene, and strangers of Rome, Jews and proselytes, Cretes and Arabians, we do hear them speak in our tongue the wonderful works of God' (Acts 2:9-11).

Though we never forget the three thousand souls added to the church in one day (Acts 2:41) this must be visualized merely as a beginning. For as the New Testament church prayed on, and preached on, God gave them more and more souls as the result of their evangelistic enterprise. They never forgot the lesson learnt at Pentecost, that power from heaven is dependent upon prayer on earth. And that power must never be squandered on self, but used to serve others, supremely by preaching to their immortal souls. Nothing stopped this onward march of the newly em-powered church. When opposition came it merely drove the church back to the throne of God. Natural, as well as spiritual, phenomena sometimes accompanied their answer. Such was the case when they had been forbidden by the powers that be to continue to preach the gospel. After they had resorted to prayer, 'the place was shaken where they were assembled together; and they were all filled with the Holy Ghost, and they spake the word of God with boldness'. Incidentally, on this occasion they certainly did not pray for this spectacular occurrence, nor in fact to be filled with the Holy Spirit, but rather that they might 'with all boldness' speak the Word of God (Acts 4:29). The demonstration of power that accompanied their preaching in answer to prayer was truly amazing. For there was nothing less than a 'multitude of them that believed'. This was accomplished when the power of God honoured the preaching of the greatest event in the world's history, namely the resurrection of the Lord Jesus Christ. For it is recorded for posterity: 'And with great power gave the apostles witness of the resurrection of the Lord Jesus: and great grace was upon them all.'

How we need, in our age, such a visitation of God! Yet God can give, not only a new age of great preachers, but a new age of great power. But both are dependent upon a new age of praying men and women who again will have 'power with God and with men' because they have 'prevailed'.

## Prayer for the lost

Finally, we need a God-given burden of prayer for the lost souls of men. We have already seen that the three thousand souls won for God at Pentecost were the fruit of a ten-day prayer meeting. Again the entrance of the gospel into Europe in general, and into Greece in particular, was a direct result of that ladies' riverside prayer meeting in Philippi 'where prayer was wont to be made' (Acts 16:13). Surely, these praying women knew the value of a soul. How we need to pray, 'O teach me the value of a soul'! And does not Christ answer us, 'What shall it profit a man if he gain the whole world and lose his own soul?' Soul-value and prayer-value should hang and hold together in a true prayer warrior of God. Have we forgotten that George Whitefield actually prayed, 'Give me souls or take my soul'? Edward Payson clearly felt the same God-given burden when he humbly confessed, 'I do not believe that my desires for a revival were over half so strong as they ought to be; nor do I see how a minister can help being in a "constant fever" when his Master is dishonoured and souls are destroyed in so many ways.'

Surely there can be no greater prayer, embracing lost man world-wide, than the words which God originally addressed to King David, but ultimately to the King of kings, the Lord Jesus Christ: 'Ask of Me, and I shall give thee the heathen for thine inheritance, and the uttermost parts of the earth for thy possession' (Ps. 2:8). Is this not part of the ongoing ministry of intercession of Christ for the lost world? Is this not the outworking of His heavenly high-priestly activity? 'This Man, because he continueth ever, hath an unchangeable priesthood. Wherefore he is able also to save them to the uttermost that come unto God by him, seeing he ever liveth to make intercession for them' (Heb. 7:24,25). Is it not wonderful that the heathen in the truest sense are already the inheritance of Christ? They are His rightful possession, purchased by His own precious blood. How encouraging that His prayers embrace the heathen, those out of every tongue, tribe and nation! Also how wonderful that the influence of prayer reaches to the limits of the universe, even to 'the uttermost parts of the earth'!

But since we are members of Christ; one with Christ in mission, surely this is a prayer He has left us to pray for the evangelization of the world. In other words, He has not merely told us with His last words that we are to preach and be witnesses unto the 'uttermost parts of the earth' (Acts 1:8), but that we are to pray for the 'uttermost parts of the earth'. We must believe with great assurance that God-given prayer and preaching will make the heathen become literally the inheritance of Christ, who says that 'he shall see of the travail of his soul, and shall be satisfied' (Isa. 53:11). This will bring to us an assurance of the certainty of success in the evangelization of the world, whatever the continent, however seemingly impossible the task, and however great the opposition with which we are faced. God asks us to pray that the heathen become the inheritance of Christ, even while 'the heathen rage' and 'the people imagine a vain thing', even while 'the kings of the earth set themselves and the rulers take counsel together, against the Lord, and against His anointed' (Ps. 2:1,2). Even when their desire is for our destruction, our desire and our prayer must be for their salvation. Have we not just seen that the early church was not surprised by the opposition to their evangelistic ventures? They in fact quoted this psalm to God in prayer, as if to remind Him, 'This is what has been predicted, but we know that this will not thwart Your purposes' (Acts 4:24-28). They knew ultimately that their opposition was 'of a truth against thy holy child Jesus' and that the rulers, the opposers and persecutors of gospel preachers, could do no more than God's 'counsel determined before to be done'. Did they not above all else recall Christ's great promise: 'I will build my church; and the gates of hell shall not prevail against it'? (Matt. 16:18.)

Let us constantly bring this great petition before God in our private and public prayer meetings: 'Ask of Me, and I shall give thee the heathen for thine inheritance, and the uttermost parts of the earth for thy possession.' Sometimes it is not possible to speak to men for God, but it is always possible to speak to God for men. How amazing that a man on his knees before the throne of God can reach the whole world for God! He can reach more men than even a satellite or any other modern invention of communication. He can reach, through the throne, into Siberia and China, behind so-called iron and bamboo curtains. In this way the heathen shall become Christ's inheritance and the uttermost parts of the earth shall bend their knees to Christ. There will be people in heaven whom we never met or witnessed to on earth, but who will be there directly as a result of our prayers. In prayer, we can, as it were, enter countries for God, where the raging heathen and the kings of the earth refuse us passports to enter. Was not this petition in the second psalm restated in the petition in the Lord's prayer in the New Testament: 'Thy kingdom come'? Let us constantly plead before God these great prayers of world-wide dimension!

E.M. Bounds in his largely forgotten classic *Purpose in Prayer* writes, 'When we calmly reflect upon the fact that the progress of our Lord's kingdom is dependent upon prayer, it is sad to think that we give so little time to the holy exercise.' Yet at the time of the Reformation we hear John Knox 'the man who made Scotland' pray, 'Give me Scotland or I die.' And John Welch, the son-in-law of Knox, was often found by his wife lying on the ground in the night weeping. He used to spend seven or eight hours a day in prayer to God. His wife used to fear for his health in the cold of the night. But he would merely draw his plaid around him and declare, 'O woman I have the souls of three thousand to answer for, and I know not how it is with many of them!'

This God-given vision of a lost world led David Brainerd, a twenty-three year old American preacher to the North American Indians, to write in his diary on 19 April 1742, 'God enabled me so to agonize in prayer that I was quite wet with sweat though in the shade and the wind cool. My soul was drawn out very much for the world. I gasped for multitudes of souls. I think I had more enlargement for sinners than for the children of God. I felt as if I could spend my life in cries for both.' Surely God-given vision and compassion for a lost world will likewise enlarge our prayer vision. Those men clearly believed what Bounds believed: 'Prayer can do anything God can do.'

## Prayer for the glory of God

If the burden of this book has been to remind us of the God-given provision for the evangelization of our lost world before it is too late, let us realize above all else that the final purpose of all our prayers and preaching is not the salvation of immortal souls, nor even the establishing of local evangelical churches, but rather the glory of God. To glorify God in evangelism is to finish the work which God has given us to do. That great evangelist to the New Hebrides, John Paton, realized that he was immortal until his work was done.

Let our last picture be of the One who combines in His glorious person both the message of the gospel and the office of the evangelist. We are privileged to enter into His prayer life at the end of His ministry, as He looks up into heaven and into His Father's face and declares, 'I have glorified thee on the earth: I have finished the work which thou gavest me to do' (John 17:4). How often we merely use the word 'glory' as a full stop at the end of our prayers! Let us rather realize that we shall never glorify God until we finish the work God has given us to do for Him in this world, and that includes the work of evangelism.